CHARACTERS

Cultural stories revealed through typography

CHARACTERS

Cultural stories revealed through typography

STEPHEN BANHAM

Foreword by Rick Poynor

Thames & Hudson | State Library of Victoria

First published in Australia in 2011
by Thames & Hudson Australia Pty Ltd
11 Central Boulevard Portside Business Park
Port Melbourne Victoria 3207
ABN: 72 004 751 964

www.thameshudson.com.au

Published in association with the
State Library of Victoria
328 Swanston Street
Melbourne Victoria 3000 Australia
slv.vic.gov.au

© Stephen Banham

ISBN: 978 050050 026 2

National Library of Australia
Cataloguing-in-Publication entry

Banham, Stephen

Characters : cultural stories revealed through typography /
Stephen Banham.
9780500500262 (hbk.)
Graphic design (Typography)
Visual communication.
655.2

Every effort has been made to trace accurate ownership
of copyright text and visual materials used in this book.
Errors or omissions will be corrected in subsequent
editions, provided notification is sent to the publisher.

EDITING
Margaret Trudgeon

INDEXER
Russell Brooks

RESEARCHER & ASSISTANT
Christine Eid

DESIGN
Letterbox

PRODUCTION
Imago Australia Pty Ltd

Printed and bound in Singapore

FOR THE TYPE-NERDS
Text Face: *Skolar Regular*
Headline Face: *Etica Extra Bold*
Cover Title Face: *Gordon Black*

FOR MORE INFORMATION
characters.net.au

ENDPAPERS
A typographic pattern composed of a script 'œ' ligature, made by English schoolchildren (c.1939) from *Writing & Writing Patterns, Book V* by Marion Richardson, University of London Press.

PAGE 2
Photomontage of Melbourne architectural signage. slide (n.d)
Image: Royal Historical Society of Victoria

OPPOSITE
Sign from Queen Victoria Market, Market Square. City of Melbourne Engineering Branch (1971) Polaroid photograph
Image: City of Melbourne Art and Heritage Collection

PAGE 6
Detail of article from 'Lighting Melbourne's sky line', *The Age* 22 May 1936, p. 3
Image: State Library of Victoria Newspapers Collection

A scene in the metal working shop, where the metal frameworks for the signs are made.

FOR CHRISTINE & KARL

CHARA

By Rick Poynor

A while ago, I took the train from Dún Laoghaire into Dublin. At Pearse Station, where I had never alighted before, on my way to the exit, an old advertisement caught my eye and I stopped to take a look at it. This was partly due to the ad's strange setting. It was off to one side of the walkway down from the platforms, behind railings in one of those pockets of fenced-off, disused and messy looking space that can form over time as large buildings are modified and extended.

A big wooden frame, many decades old, was recessed into the brick wall. This structure was clearly no longer used for contemporary advertising, but amazingly it still had an old, abandoned ad in it – a poster with torn and peeling edges. The image was purely typographic, in red on a dirty white background, and it simply said, 'Cadbury's Chocolate ... Delicious Wholesome ... Always ask for Cadbury's'. This legend was enclosed by a heavy black rule. I couldn't date the poster with any accuracy, though it was probably from the 1920s or earlier. The 'Delicious Wholesome' part was picked out in a slightly crude script and there were some pleasing oddities of sizing and placement.

Perhaps other posters had been pasted on top, sealing the Cadbury's poster inside, and this was the reason why it had survived for so long. A few black lowercase letters – a, c and e – and the light-blue background from another old poster showed through gashes in its surface. Its historical value and visual appeal were obvious, but maybe when it came to light the station's officials decided to leave it where it was, preserved in its own informal museum with a measure of protection from the fence. This did seem a little casual, though anyone can now pause, as I did, to puzzle over it, charmed by this unexpected interlude of alphabetical time travel. Later, I found a statement from an artist on Flickr, claiming that he had painted the poster for a TV production in 2000 titled *Rebel Heart*, which was filmed at Pearse Station. He was astonished to learn that it is still there. The poster is, however, a copy of an original Cadbury's design.

If the poster were in Melbourne, I have no doubt that Stephen Banham would have noticed it, cherished it, photographed it, found out as much of its history as he could, and put it in this book.

I salute his mission as a typo-archaeologist. What he suggests is true: there is a way of paying close attention to letters in the urban environment that can be applied wherever one happens to be; and the poetry and pleasure of these typographic markers improves as they age, like wine in the bottle. Not long ago, in Melbourne, Stephen told me about the secret lettering in the Centreway Arcade (page 28). Before I left, I had to see it for myself. Not knowing the city well, I had trouble finding the wall and nearly gave up. When I did eventually locate the grid of metal letters, I had the feeling of being privy to a thrilling act of subterfuge. These signs, inscriptions and codes are everywhere. Go and find them.

Rick Poynor writes about design and visual culture. His books include *Obey the Giant: Life in the Image World* (Birkhauser, 2001) and *No More Rules: Graphic Design and Postmodernism* (Laurence King, 2003).

Learning to spell

'At the age of three I spelled my first word of five letters: Aspro. That was because there was a big electrical sign that winked on and off on the south bank of the Yarra spelling out A-S-P-R-O, ASPRO, day and night'.[1]

DAME PHYLLIS FROST

Who we are, letter by letter

We walk past them every day, possibly not even noticing them, but they are part of our lives and the history of whatever city we happen to live in. Typographic signs, some dating back nearly a century, some brand new, all have stories to tell.

This book reveals how the life of a city can be viewed through its letterforms, and more specifically, the most public of all typography, its signage. However, this lens could be focused on any city, in any country, anywhere in the world. The places, experiences and stories related here are unique to Melbourne, Australia, but the 'way of seeing' signs is as universal as the human appeal of storytelling. Rather than presenting the new, I hope to offer a new way of looking at the familiar.

The following pages present a selection of signs seen around a city – in this case, Melbourne – that have helped to shape its character. Some have long since been pulled down and discarded, existing now only in photographs or design sketches. Some have been preserved by dedicated locals and have either been given a new lease of life or are sitting in a warehouse somewhere waiting for a new incarnation. Some are still new, in use and relevant to modern city life.

As you flick through this book you might see images of signs that you remember from your childhood or from driving home across the Yarra River late at night. Most Melbournians will be familiar with the Skipping Girl sign and the Nylex sign, as well as those that have lit up busy intersections at St Kilda and Oakleigh for many years. Less well known to some are the signs that have disappeared from view as buildings have been demolished, or signs that have

been painted or boarded over. Some less imposing signs sit patiently waiting to be noticed by passers-by; others live on in people's memories, despite having disappeared years ago. These signs are all a part of the life and character of a city, and each has its own story to tell.

Typographic storytelling links and interweaves stories of social change, politics and economics – factors often considered external to graphic design. Telling our cultural stories in this way links the multiple design disciplines into a single social fabric – drawing threads from all sorts of areas, including architecture, industrial design and fashion design. The public is now comfortable with such connections, thanks to the familiar language of a networked online world. In bringing these together, it is not so much a case of creating the stories behind our designed environment, but of simply seeing them and relating them to a larger cultural experience.

PAGE 15
Butcher shop window
(1969) *Image: Angus
O'Callaghan from
'Marvellous Melbourne'
Collection. Courtesy
Kozminsky Gallery*

LEFT TOP
The much sought after
tram rolls of Melbourne
(2011) *Image: Lan Huang.
Courtesy of Letterbox*

MIDDLE
Olunda homewares taking
pride of place in Ikea,
Richmond (2011)
Image: Author

BOTTOM
Typography hits the
high street. Typo store,
Melbourne Central (2011)
*Image: Lan Huang
Courtesy of Letterbox*

This interest in a city's typography reaches into all sorts of areas. For instance, on a recent trip to my local IKEA store I was given an added surprise. There in the wall-hanging section, in among the dramatic landscapes designed to match the sofas, was something that really caught my eye. Although not the kind of thing you would expect in this store environment, it was also strangely familiar. It was a framed alphabet – not a child's alphabet in bright bubble writing, but a very adult alphabet, all in capital letters, using sans serif type, akin to *Akzidenz Grotesk*.[1] This neatly framed homeware item, by the name of Olunda, was presented like a well-preserved type specimen page from the early twentieth century. To my surprise it contained highlighted letters in red that didn't even spell out a naff statement – instead they consisted of the vowels and a Y. But somewhere along the way the context had changed. What would once have been displayed only on the walls of a graphic design studio had now become an item of popular domestic decor to be placed in a bedroom or living room.

It shouldn't really have come as such a surprise. The past few years has seen the popular emergence of letters on many retail store shelves. Whereas once the only letters available were brightly painted wooden capital letters to spell out a child's name on their bedroom door, now there is a very distinct mainstream interest in letterforms of all shapes, sizes and colours. Fashion retailer Cotton On recently branched out to establish a chain of stores under the name Typo. Across dozens of stores nationwide, Typo offers hundreds of items (mostly using letterforms), bringing mainstream interest in letterforms into our living rooms, kitchens, bedrooms, bathrooms, and just about everywhere else. In the store's own words: 'Typo is a one-stop concept store ... taking trends from the fashion industry and applying them to notebooks, decal wall art, gift wrap and other specialty items. Typo offers products with attitude ...'[2]

Running in tandem with this, the last few years has also seen an increase in the availability of used and vintage signage. While many of these are original artefacts salvaged from buildings due for demolition, others are 'mock signage' – new objects that have been created to look like real signage, even down to an artificially distressed appearance to appear rusted and faded. Signage is now become an object of mainstream desire.

So how did this come about? The answer may lie in how we relate to signage letterforms. Not only do they offer us a way of remembering and giving meaning to a place, but they are also an expression of ourselves. There is a certain irony to be enjoyed here. Through a desire for 'authenticity', buyers of old signage are purchasing instant heritage; a back story to be recounted to friends and family. Often it is less about the actual artefact (such as a huge old metal letter N) than about the perceived character and narrative one imagines accompanies it

TOP

Hook turn tea-towel
by Make Me Iconic (2010).
Considered a unique icon
of Melbourne, the Right
Turn From Left Only was
first introduced in 1916
to keep increasingly
congested intersections
clear for trams. The move
is an exercise in timing,
skill and judgement.
*Image: Courtesy of Make
Me Iconic*

BOTTOM

Tram roll cards by
Poulier & Poulier (2010)
Image: Lan Huang
Courtesy of Letterbox

(*Oh that, yeah. I found it one night in an abandoned factory in Newport*').

The 'cultural mainstreaming' of typography has arrived. People now feel comfortable discussing typefaces in everyday conversation. No longer the esoteric language of the printing and publishing trade, everybody has an opinion (or many) on the letters that surround us. They are now broadly accepted as a part of our everyday lives. And with this the acknowledgement that they are a part of us, an expressive ingredient of our culture.

The rising presence of typographic products in the retail environment is the most explicit step in this acknowledgement, aligning its 'cultural worth' with a corresponding 'commercial worth'.

One of the most popular local typographic motifs is the Melbourne tram roll. Harking back to a pre-digital age of W-class trams, these super-long, hand-painted fabric rolls were once used to display the names of Melbourne's various tram route destinations. At the end of each tram trip the roll would be manually rotated by the conductor to show its return destination or perhaps a new one, boldly presented in white type on a black background, in the rectangular strip window at the front of the tram. Original rolls are now highly sought after, particularly in their city of origin. But for those not able to afford an original Melbourne tram roll there is a plethora of replicas now available, ranging from the typographically accurate through to the downright

unconvincing. Recent tram roll homewares have included postcards, tea towels and framed canvas prints.

Local homeware designer, Make Me Iconic, has found a great deal of inspiration in local signage, reproducing the Nylex sign, the Skipping Girl Vinegar sign, a Milk Bar sign and even a hook-turn traffic sign (a peculiar road turn specific to Melbourne) onto a range of homeware items. When asked why she chose such motifs for her products, the founder of Make Me Iconic, Natasha Skunca, reflected:

After being away from Melbourne for 10 years, the Nylex building visually represented to me that I was home again. My heart still skips a beat every time I see it. We don't have an Opera House or Harbour Bridge here like Sydney. Melbourne is not that glamorous or obvious. Melbourne is more about secret discoveries and unsung glamour, and to me the Nylex building represents that.[3]

So buying a Nylex Sign tea towel isn't just about liking that specific sign, it is a proud link between our identity and the cultural memory of an entire city.

People like letters and they want to celebrate them. Some marketers have been quick to pick up on this. Flipping through the newspaper real estate section, the lush images of inner-city apartments invariably feature walls covered in large letters and signage, their graphic presence at times even threatening the supremacy of the headline. And if an apartment is not so photogenic, simply use some local signage as a readily

recognisable landmark. This cleverly sells a desirable urban lifestyle by using the most immediate visual shorthand for that place, signage.

So what does all this say about us? It says that the signage and letterforms we see every day has the effect of creating cultural markers of location and memory in our lives. For many this will be consciously recognised, while for others it may operate at an almost subliminal level. This essential human need for a sense of 'real' geographic location maintains a counter to the 'placelessness' of much modern media, particularly the internet. As our daily lives are increasingly exposed to anybody, anytime, anywhere, the importance of 'place' to our sense of personal identity is balanced by a more localised culture, expressing our own specific and unique environments and experiences.

Keeping it real (or not)

Anybody going into Joe's Shoe Store in Northcote with a pair of old shoes in need of repair will get a bit of a surprise. Instead of being greeted by a wall of footwear, repair tools and equipment, they will discover a long line of wine and beer bottles. Instead of the shoe-fitting area, there is now a row of drinking booths. It is a bar. Everything has changed – or has it?

Out in the street the signage still boldly states Joe's Shoe Store in a strong sans serif type, followed by the words 'Australian and Continental' in script.

As *The Age* newspaper remarked:

The unenlightened might sneer at a new bar brazenly co-opting the name of the business that preceded it, accusing it of being unimaginative or even lazy, but this is recycling of the highest order.[4]

But there is more in this sentiment than just recycling; it is part of a bigger current desire to preserve a historical lineage, a continuity of our sense of place.

But, of course, the owners of Joe's Shoe Store are not alone in seeing the value of retaining identity through signage. When The Recorded Music Salon at the boutique end of Collins Street closed down the premises were also converted into a bar. Although the old, dusty tape recorders and turntables were no longer displayed in the front window, the distinctive gold script of the signage was retained and the bar was appropriately named The Recorded Music Salon for some time.

Others have taken a more playful response to maintaining a link to heritage through their use of pre-existing signage. Although the interior of Collingwood's Ilk Bar features many artful depictions of the sound-alike 'elk', the name of the bar was not inspired by this species of deer but instead derived from the original external signage.

Occupying what was once a milk bar, the letter M had fallen off the signage, leaving the now renowned Ilk Bar.

TOP
Letters for everybody.
Playful use of raised
alphabet in the Flagstaff
Gardens playground
(2007) *Image: Author*

BOTTOM LEFT
The on-street marketing
of the Ark Apartments,
Bridge Road, Richmond
(2010) *Image: Author*

BOTTOM RIGHT
The happy domestic
co-existence with
brandy advertising,
North Melbourne (2010)
*Image: Lan Huang
Courtesy of Letterbox*

So you think you're pretty spacial: Architects and typographers

Typography has more in common with architecture than many architects would care to admit. It is not surprising that there is a latent mutual attraction between typography and architectural form: both typographers and architects talk about grids and stratification, proportion and visible stability, and about how to organise light and dark.[5] Both represent a strong and succinct visual language through their structure, geometry and proportion. Both forms share a fundamental relationship with human scale, with architectural 'sight lines' and typographic 'legibility' both representing clarity of design.

Architecture provides an immediate point of reference in the telling of human culture, both ancient and present. It can be read as a text, and typography can also be presented as a physical experience, thus taking centre stage and acquiring a sculptural presence.[6] When we build type in three-dimensional form or at a monumental scale the potent relationship between architecture and typography becomes even stronger. Indeed, the original definition of the term 'typotecture' is: 'type actually being able to subject itself to gravity and acquire a physical presence, to expand into a space and come closer to architectural form'.[7]

Both architecture and typography run happily in tandem with techno-logical advancement. While classical typographic forms were once chiselled

into the façades of buildings, modernity brought with it distinct opportunities to create geometric forms that were fundamentally more architectural. The typefaces chosen, sans serif and exclusively using capital letters, fitted in with this idea. This formal limitation is still around today, probably because it conveys the physical quality of architecture more directly.[8]

Architects often resist signage, boldly claiming that the building does not need signage 'because the building is the sign'. And although this may be true for a small number of emblematic buildings, it is doubtful that the public view their city in such a way. Just as the buildings that surround us help to create our mental recollection of a place, letterforms also emboss themselves upon our memory of place. The relationship between the built and the typographic is etched deep into the multi-layered history of a city. Sometimes when one is erased, the other

emerges. Packed tightly together along the streetscape a demolished building will often unearth signage written upon its neighbour, yielding once more its paint-thin layer of cultural history to passers-by.

For artist Michelle Hamer, coming from an architectural background has informed her view of signage:

Signage fascinates me. I see it everywhere. I'm interested in the spaces it occupies. What would have been there if the sign was not there? These spaces are often unused and are yet necessary as well ... Signage is powerful because it reflects on and promotes our cultural edicts. It's an instructional language that reflects our belief systems. It's a language of faith – from judgement ('If you drink and drive you're a bloody idiot') to aspiration ('Is this your new home?'). Whereas once people may have looked to religion for such instruction, there are now other languages. These are messages we can

relate to. You could call signage 'the new, new Testament'.[9]

In her earlier work, Hamer addressed the digital language of roadside-warning signage. Sometimes these units would malfunction, producing odd, fractured messages, which she captured as meticulously crafted tapestries. 'I'm interested in these margins of error – by being digital yet malfunctioning they have their own life and humanity – almost being anthropomorphic.'[10]

Recently, Hamer's work has referenced commercial signage, mostly real estate boards, located on the ever-expanding outer-suburban fringe. Once you begin to interpret this signage as messages of faith, their aspirational intent becomes more transparent. 'Put yourself in a better place' could be as much a spiritual statement as it is about physical relocation.

Hamer's unique perspective, presented through the unlikely medium of tapestry,

PAGE 20
... *ill* (2005)
Michelle Hamer
hand-stitched tapestry
on perforated plastic
26.5 × 34 cm
*All images courtesy
of artist*

PAGE 21
TOP (LEFT TO RIGHT)
Speed kills (2005)
... *your* (2005)
Today (2005)
Wipe out five (2005)
Michelle Hamer

Hand-stitched tapestry
on perforated plastic
26.5 × 34 cm

PAGE 21
BOTTOM (LEFT TO RIGHT)
Arrive Alive (2005)
Slow down (2005)
Fatigue kills (2005)
Blocked out (2005)
Michelle Hamer.
Hand-stitched tapestry
on perforated plastic
26.5 × 34 cm

BELOW
She'll be Right (2009)
Jon Campbell
enamel, MDF, 13 pieces
each 210 × 120 cm
*Image: Courtesy of Darren
Knight Gallery, Sydney and
Kalimanrawlins Gallery,
Melbourne*

makes for a deceivingly sharp commentary, not only on the messages around us but on our role as viewers.

The artworks of Jon Campbell also employ the visual language of signage, but in a more direct way. 'Signage is part of the visual fabric of a neighbour-hood. Even though most people take it for granted, it's always there and is particular to that place.'[11] The suggestion of a sense of identity through locality is central to much of his work – be it national or the local community. It also offers the work a point of difference and

purpose. 'We [artists] all have the same stuff, the same equipment, so we have to decide what is going to make [our] contribution unique. A space for what I am interested in.'[12]

His works embed single words or phrases within the familiar language of the corner milk bar or fish and chip shop. Some works use phrases reflecting unique Australian colloquialisms: *She'll be right, Snot block, Up shit creek*; others address local concerns – *Save our pool*, while others reference pop music ephemera, such as concert playlists

and posters, seen in *I wanna be in The Go-Betweens*. This raw, vernacular language is then reborn as painted form on display, completing a kind of loop that reinstates the sign once again. As Campbell remarks, 'The artwork directs the viewer back outside for them to look at things (signage) differently.'[13]

Like the art gallery, the experience of looking at signage within a sequenced set of printed pages (i.e. this book) is, of course, an artificial one. Although no book can hope to replace the experience of seeing signage in its true physical

context, the imagery contained here has included the street surrounds wherever possible, and page sequences have been mindful of offering unexpected discoveries for the reader.

Considering the dynamic complexity of urban environments, the signage that is featured in the book is but a small selection of what is out there, chosen for the stories and social significance each sign offers. By no means is this meant to represent a complete and exhaustive list; it is, in fact, an open invitation to others to add their own stories and experiences

to this collective narrative, expanding the discussion beyond mere paper and ink. Our urban environments change every day and with it, their typographic voices. The removal of one site is then counter-balanced by the emergence of a new one – or perhaps not.

For many people the first thing that comes to mind when discussing typography in an urban environment is graffiti. Its absence from these pages is a result of a deliberate and considered focus. Graffiti (from tagging to stenciling) has become a highly discussed and documented aspect

of Melbourne in recent years, resulting in numerous books on graffiti culture (including some by this very publisher), which comprehensively address this phenomena.

Leaving graffiti aside not only avoids duplication, but sharpens the focus onto a less explored perspective, the typography of signage. Rather than discounting the significant cultural contribution of graffiti, the diversity of letterforms featured here adds to and complements the already documented culture of graffiti.

Possible futures of signage

Less is less

To get a total sense of the social and cultural role signage plays in our lives it really has to be seen as a continuum (past, present, future), as well as being viewed in tandem with other forms of cultural expression. Although the vast majority of 'signage spectaculars' were lost during a period when such structures were considered 'visual pollution' and a symbol of an ugly 'featurism', the public appreciation of its heritage and cultural significance has since become more sophisticated.

Like the city itself, advertising media is dynamic. The age of neon lent itself to an earlier and cruder world of 'mass' advertising, when the idea of displaying a fixed single message to a mass audience was considered appropriate and effective. However, we now live in the age of finely segmented media, where niche markets are addressed by customised messages; where users not only absorb but contribute to media messages and in the process build 'brand relationships' and 'brand cultures' around a product or service. Through more finely targeted marketing, the media landscape has been completely transformed, and with it, our visual landscape.

Digital technologies allowing viewer interaction have turned what was once an advertising monologue into something more akin to a consumer dialogue.

OPPOSITE
The Florence Avenue
signage for Corbett Lyon's
Lyon Housemuseum
*Image: Courtesy Lyons
and Lyon Housemuseum,
photographer Dianna Snape*

BELOW LEFT
The Young and Jackson
Hotel façade (c. 1967)
photograph, gelatin silver
*Image: State Library of
Victoria Pictures Collection*
H2004.101/153A
*Courtesy of the Herald
& Weekly Times Pty Ltd*

BELOW RIGHT
The Young and Jackson
Hotel façade (c. 2009)
Image: Nick Kreisler

PAGE 26
A digital depiction of the
roof typography at the
Lyon Housemuseum.
*Image Courtesy Lyons
and Lyon Housemuseum*

This has made the investment of a huge, fixed and static advertising medium less viable. In combination with a wave of public distain for their presence on the city skylines, large-scale signage became threatened species. When comparing images of mid-twentieth century Melbourne and the city as it is today, one thing becomes immediately apparent – typographic signage has far less presence now than it did 50 years ago. Tightly controlled by civic regulations or consolidated into boxed multi-message mediums, urban advertising is neater and more orderly now than ever before.

The future of signage can be seen surrounding the roof of the Young and Jackson Hotel at the intersection of Flinders and Swanston Streets in Melbourne's CBD. Having been used as a popular advertising space for almost all of Melbourne's life, the vast array of signage that once covered every flat surface of the hotel has now been rolled into a single unit, a huge electronic message display (EMD) that wraps right around the hotel roofline like an illuminated crown. Unlike static media, this (highly profitable) display presents constantly dynamic content and news feeds. It offers future possibilities of content that is able to be completely personalised or even respond to temperature or traffic conditions. The single message is dead.

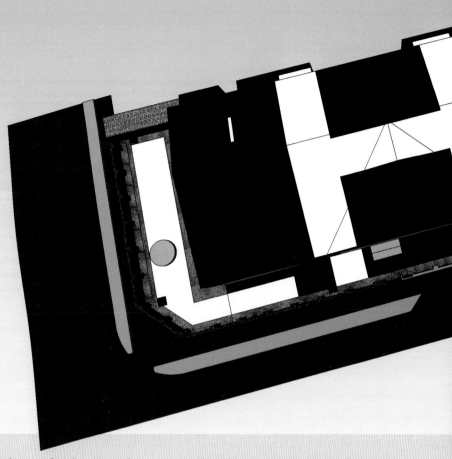

Possible futures of signage

From the top

It is not only the speed and variety of messages that are changing, but the entire perspective altogether. Signage, once designed for a mid-20th century viewing position, from the street (or motor car), is being reconfigured to accommodate viewing from a completely different perspective – space.

When the architect and art collector Corbett Lyon designed the signage for his recently established Lyon Housemuseum, the signage was considered from a much larger perspective:

The idea was about how we connect this small museum in Kew, a suburb in Australia, to other museums around the world through the kind of global view afforded by Google Earth. So we've written out the initials of the museum L, H and M in capital letters laid out across the site, so that the building sits on this ... and it made the garden design very easy as well.[14]

Worldwide digital mapping and Global Positioning Systems (GPS) offer the field of signage a new and exciting language that carries with it possibilities for instant searchability, dynamic content and graphic visibility from far above. Expanding beyond the traditionally 'topographical' signage associated with helicopter landing pads, bank security vans or outback cattle stations, this new satellite signage will paradoxically be seeking to locate something using the

'placeless' technology of the internet.

This significant shift in orientation brings with it a whole new way of navigating our cities. Instead of looking *horizontally* across a cityscape for familiar signs and directions, we are now looking *downwards* at our personal mobile screens.

Symbolically, the sources of illumination have changed – the lively flashing globes or coloured neon tubes that we once associated with a lively city are moving to smaller, personal sources of light, the handheld screens with which we seek to find our way through our cities.

The demand for ever-changing content makes the re-emergence of static, monolithic landmark signage unlikely. Instead, digital technologies will continue to exploit the strong relationship between typography and the built environment.

Perhaps the most insightful observation should be left to an uncannily precise prediction made by English signage designer Jock Kinneir over 30 years ago:

The chief stumbling block ... inflexibility – no longer holds true, and buildings which are already complex environmental systems could ... become public communication systems with a capacity for constant and immediate updating. All that is necessary is to grasp the concept that communication is in some cases of equal importance to shelter.[15]

Cleverly concealed words of subversion. Signage that can only be read from certain angles. This is the hidden language of Melbourne's laneways.

Looking inwards

Once used as access for trade deliveries, rubbish removal and even sewage cartage, Melbourne's network of laneways is now widely celebrated as a unique cultural aspect of a flatly gridded central city that otherwise lacks the natural beauty of its nearest rival, Sydney. However, these laneways hold other secrets and stories in their typography, showing that true beauty is to be found in the details, the folds, crevices and shadows.

Perhaps one of the most popular of these pedestrian thoroughfares runs between Collins Street and Flinders Lane. Comprising two distinct halves, Centre Place and Centreway Arcade became one of the 'first generation of revitalised laneways' in the 1980s when the City of Melbourne urban designers and planners 'moved to protect and upgrade the city's remaining laneways and alleys, encouraging small retailers to move into the city and take spaces facing the street rather than looking inwards'.[1]

Centreway's fashionable connection to the 'art precinct' of Flinders Lane has made it a favoured place for bustling lunchtime crowds, film crews, fashion shoots and, of course, hordes of curious tourists. The ever-changing spectacle of rich and colourful graffiti is also a strong focus of attention, making it one of Melbourne's most photographed laneways.

A similar cultural revival of the Centreway Arcade end may well have been hindered by the extensive architectural renovations carried out in the 1980s by Cocks, Carmichael and Whitford.[2] Although this refashioning, featuring angled, colourful geometry and its central multistorey atrium, may not have aged gracefully, it has created one of the most ironic and well-hidden typographic statements in the entire city.

On the southern end of the arcade, high above eye-level of passing shoppers and pedestrians, is a wall evenly studded with a pattern. On closer observation one can see that this continuous pattern is made up of metal uppercase letters. If you take the time to read and decipher these letters into words the wall reveals its intended message: *We live in a society that sets an inordinate value on consumer goods and services*. The irony is immediate. Built into the very architectural structure of a shopping arcade, this is pure subversion. Spoken through the calm typographic voice of modernity (the typeface *Helvetica*) and cloaked as a monotonous visual pattern, this contradictory and provocative statement is amplified to those who not only care to *look* but who care to *read*.

All that glitters is not legible
One of the most recent additions to Melbourne's laneway urban renewal is Goldsbrough Lane. Drawing upon the 'gold' theme, the lane's signage is presented as lumpy nuggets playfully floating above the pedestrian.

As the viewer approaches, it becomes apparent that the letters are in fact scattered across a series of wires, the entire title only becoming completely legible when seen from the front.

OPPOSITE
Political subversion lies just below a cold exterior in Centreway Arcade (2009) *Image: Nick Kreisler*

ABOVE
The uniquely 'gold-themed' signage for Goldsbrough Lane (2011) *Image: Lan Huang Courtesy of Letterbox*

LEFT
Port Phillip Arcade
in better times (1969)
Wolfgang Sievers
photograph, gelatin silver
Image: State Library of
Victoria Pictures Collection
H98.30/215

Hidden away in North Melbourne's cobblestoned Lancashire Lane is an argument writ large in white paint for all to see. And it's all about a toilet.

A public scandal

This spirited banter, scrawled in white paint directly across the dilapidated concrete and old metal doors on the rear laneway wall of the property, concerns the maintenance – or lack of – of a tenant's toilet. The result is a public typographic delight. The dispute even features a painted illustration of the offending toilet with its broken pipe rendered in silhouette at near actual size.

The first few sentences appear to have been struck through and painted over, inferring a re-visiting, editing or re-consideration of the original statement. The author of this unique piece of typography is unknown, but it appears to have been written a long time ago. As for the eventual outcome of the argument, we will probably never know what happened. The tenants have long sinced moved on and the property now lies completely derelict.[1] What is left, however, is a rarely seen public protest expressed through typography. Thankfully its obscure location down a one-way lane has preserved it, but for how much longer remains uncertain. Its sheer expressiveness reminds us of the strong ability of type to graphically depict our stories, thoughts and disputes, even if they are just over a broken toilet.

Illegible in parts, the argument takes some time to comprehend. A transcript, keeping the original grammar, reads as:

FIRST DOOR

the woman told me I had to repair the pipe because they has the power to force me to fix it. my tenant told them, he saw the man with a scoop working on 4.1.95. the woman hire a Chinese to scare my tenant. My tenant scare move out 3 day later.

SECOND DOOR

the woman told me they can see the water leak by look at the small hole after I criticize them they advice the builder to cover the damage leave a small hole for you to look at. the woman told me the hole for the storm water. the pipe Rust through. the Wall cave in by itself on 4.1.95. the woman hire a Chinese to scare my tenant. my tenant so scare move out 3 days later.

SECOND DOOR

B ... should call me to see the damaged spot in front of the women, why after build the wall to cover the damaged spot then bring the women to help you.

WALL

the 2 women create a new unequal justice by help the builder. they cracked my toilet pipe, damaged wall. the builder not only refused to repair he brought 2 women to help him. they told me they has the power to force me to pay for the repair & also sue me $10,000 after I argue How the toilet wall cave in they immediate retreat & say the demolition digging foundation & load the rubbles by hand. the toilet wall cave in. crack pipe because too old.

Political banners rarely get bigger than 110 metres tall – the vertical span of a message painted down an abandoned tower that once dominated Spencer Street.

The 110-metre finger of protest

This highly effective (but illegal) use of the derelict Spencer Street Power Station tower as a massive vertical canvas for public political statement enabled the anti-logging campaign unprecedented exposure to passing city workers and residents alike. Down one side of the tower, neatly painted in white capital letters, they declared: 'No jobs on a dead planet', while another questioned: 'Why log our water catchment?' Considering the extraordinarily perilous act of executing such a statement, the authorities were understandably hesitant about taking the risk and expense of removing it from a site that was due for demolition. Instead it was left, proclaiming its message as an unintended and powerful Melbourne landmark for several years.

After being decommissioned in 1981, the Power Station site lay dormant for some time before being sold to a consortium in 2006. It has now undergone a very expensive demolition and decontamination process to clean the site before its development into another piece of prime city real estate.

WOODCHIPS (CORPORATE$) WATER (YOURS)

WHY LOG OUR WATER CATCHMENTS?

NO JOBS ON A DEAD PLANET

Something had to be done. Fitzroy Pool manager James Murphy was constantly rescuing migrant children from the deep end of the inner-city pool he ran. The year was 1953 and Fitzroy was now home to a considerable number of postwar migrants, many from Italy. James thought that there must be a better way of making them aware of the potential perils of the Olympic-size pool.

Aqua Profonda

OPPOSITE
The Aqua Profonda sign,
Fitzroy Pool (2011)
Image: Rhiannon Slatter

BELOW
The mocked-up Aqua
Profonda sign from the
film *Monkey Grip* (1982)
*Image: Courtesy of
Patricia Lovell*

Then an idea came to him. He turned to an Italian friend and asked what the words for 'deep water' were in Italian. 'Acqua profonda,' came the answer. So he had the words painted in large letters across the back wall of the pool, misspelling the Italian word 'Acqua' into the Latin 'Aqua'. The sign 'Aqua Profonda' represents a small demonstration of how migrants were becoming accepted as part of the local community; a rare, tangible example of public acknowledgement of the cultural impact of the mass migration program.[1] Whether the sign has ever helped to minimise accidents is unknown, but one thing is for sure, 'Aqua Profonda' has gone on to enter social folklore.

As well as being a symbol of Fitzroy's multicultural complexion, the sign's social significance was reinforced by its appearance in the 1977 Helen Garner novel *Monkey Grip*, and the film of the same name, made in 1982. In this tale the sign appears as the title of the first chapter, serving as a metaphor for the chaotic relationship between Nora and Javo, the two main characters.[2] A copy of the 'Aqua Profonda' sign was painted in Sydney, where much of the film was shot.

In the politically fiery period of the mid-1990s 'Aqua Profonda' became a popular catchcry for the community struggle to save the Fitzroy Pool from closure by the City of Yarra. Because of the ultimate success of the 'Save Our Pool' campaign, the tactics (and the catchcry) are now often used as a model case study in the academic study of grassroots political action.

More recently the social importance of the 'Aqua Profonda' sign has been further reinforced by the tiling of these same words (with typographic error intact) on the base of the pool, making the message visible through the waters of the deep end. Aqua Profonda has since gone on to be used as a title for everything from a local musical (with a cast of over 120 schoolchildren),[3] right through to an Australian exhibition at the 2001 Venice Biennale of Contemporary Art.

Aqua Profonda's continued representation of social equality has been recognised by Heritage Victoria, which has taken formal steps to protect this unique, culturally important and misspelt icon.

Civic
The poetry of instruction

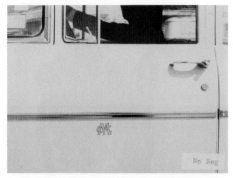

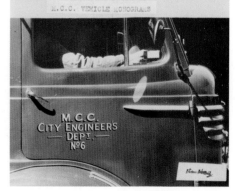

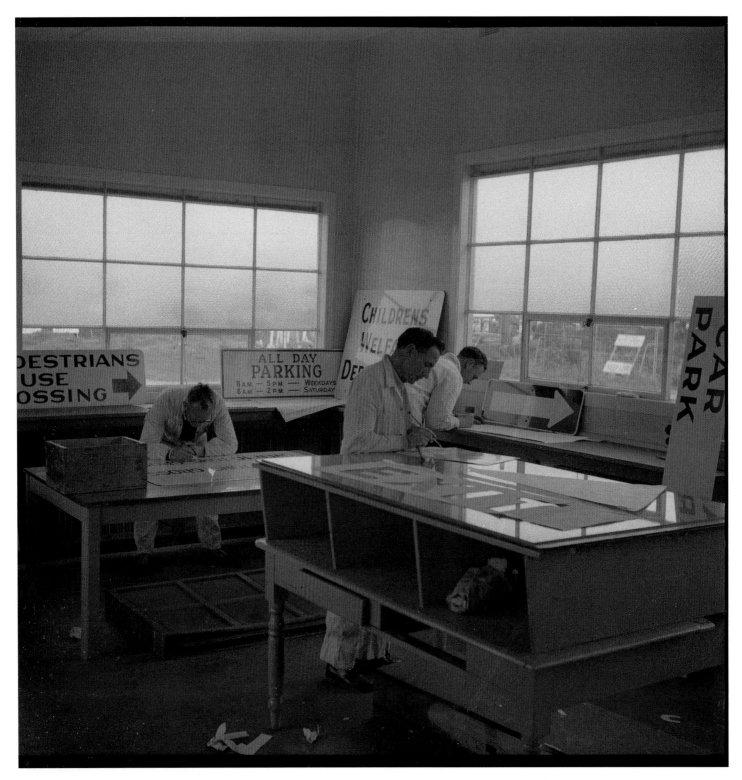

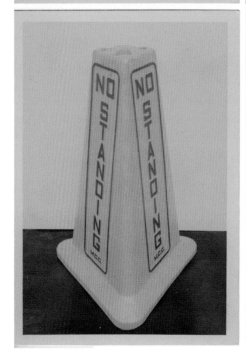

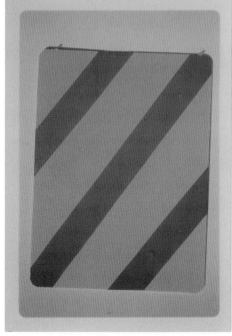

The forgotten glittering prize

On 21 April 1856 stonemasons working on the site of the University of Melbourne downed tools in protest and marched to Parliament House (which was also in the process of being built). Declaring that every worker should have 'Eight hours labour, eight hours rest and eight hours recreation', the eight-hour movement led to Melbourne building workers being among the first in the world to achieve such conditions. Until that time workers often worked 12- or even 16-hour days or more, with only one day off per week.

The timing was in their favour – inflated by goldrush wealth, a booming Melbourne needed important public buildings to be built, leading to a very high demand for building workers. This situation left the workers in a powerful position to negotiate for better wages and conditions. The victory of the eight-hour movement then moved across other industries and was eventually commemorated as the 'Eight Hour Day' (now better known as Labour Day).

By the 1880s it was decided to raise funding for a monument to the movement to be built adjacent to Parliament House, at the top of Bourke Street.

When conservators were restoring the '888' globe, a renowned union monument that typographically declares workers' rights to 'work, recreation and rest', they discovered something quite unexpected. Inside the 23-carat gold leaf globe were objects that had been slipped into it over 100 years earlier.

Its eventual construction, during the economic downturn of the 1890s, called for substantial design simplification. The initially ambitious figurative design by prominent sculptor Percival Ball was dramatically streamlined to one that was completely typographic – an elegant series of three numeral '8's and a globe, encircled by the words 'Labour, Recreation and Peace'.

In 1923 the monument was moved adjacent to Trades Hall in Carlton. It was during its restoration in 2006 to celebrate the 150th anniversary of the original struggle that the monument's globe was opened, yielding its mysterious objects. Inside the globe were two old sealed jars containing what appeared to be a union manifesto, along with some coins and medals from the period.

The meaning behind these items is open to speculation – perhaps the manifesto was slipped inside the globe not only to serve as a historical reminder of previous struggles but also to reiterate to future generations the importance of workers' rights in general.

In an odd twist of fate, we have the economic hardships of the late nineteenth century to thank for one of the city's most unique, but least recognised, typographic monuments. Instead of the more conventional figurative statue, the set of three numerals that form the 888 sculpture stand as a powerful symbol of a struggle whose social benefits have been widely shared, even by today's public, who walk past barely even noticing it.

PAGES 56, 57
AND OPPOSITE
Beautiful but forgotten;
the 888 monument,
Melbourne (2011)
*Image: 20m aerial
photograph*

Prior to the establishment of government-run universal welfare systems, friendly societies had the role of addressing many of the social needs of their communities. Membership of these societies often ran along the lines of one's occupation (guilds), religion (Christian associations) or place of birth (native associations). By the Second World War many of these friendly societies had developed comprehensive sets of products, including hospital and medical insurance, household insurance, life insurance, and personal and home loans. What many of these societies had in common – a principle of mutual self-help – was communicated through some common typographic and architectural traits.

Lighting the beacons

The age of the friendly society not only marked the genesis of the modern insurance industry, but also left behind a legacy of some monumental buildings throughout Melbourne, built to show the virtues of collective strength and reliability. The scale and verticality of both the Temperance & General Building (commonly known as the T&G Building) (c.1928) and the Manchester Unity Building (c.1932) display this confidence through their towering modernity.

Both buildings are crowned by a prominent beacon, whose multi-faceted glass panels feature their huge typographic initials, T&G and MU respectively. When illuminated by pure bright sunlight these letterforms emphasise the grand cathedral-like qualities of the buildings, ushering the Christian leadlight traditions into the age of modernity.

In fact, so well-loved by the public was the T&G Building that in 1930 it was voted 'Melbourne's most beautiful building' in a competition run by the *Herald* newspaper.

Paintings and photographs from the 1930s show these two buildings looming large over the Melbourne skyline. Although now dwarfed by modern skyscrapers, these typographic beacons symbolise the power of the collective, as well as the sturdy faith of an earlier age of commerce.

The T&G building was once dubbed the 'Tooth and Gum Building' because of the number of dentists operating within its suites. Similarly, today the Manchester Unity Building accommodates many dentists in its commercial tenancies.

BELOW
The sculpturally complex
façade of the Australian
Natives Association (ANA)
building (2009)
Image: Nick Kriesler

Perfect balance

The Australian Natives Association (ANA) was another friendly society, formed in 1871 with a specific point of difference – its membership was restricted to those born in Australia. Ironically, but indicative of the time, there was a complete absence of Aboriginal Australians among its members. The Association lobbied for Australian federation, Australian-made goods, the establishment of Australia Day, the adoption of the wattle as the national floral emblem, and was ahead of its time on many environmental issues.

Like the T&G and MU buildings, the façade of the ANA building (1939) draws heavily upon classical themes and proportions, and has a pronounced vertical emphasis. Among the more typical motifs of the period – the rising sun and the Melbourne crest flanked by the kangaroo and emu – is an impressive menagerie of native Australian fauna. But it is in the typography that the purest of classical symmetry can be found. The acronym of the association – ANA – offers a very rare typographic occurrence – an ambigram, meaning that the letterform combination is perfectly symmetrical. Such typographic happenstance is reward for the careful observer.

ANA

The ambigram of the ANA titling offers a perfectly symmetrical typographic balance.

A civic menagerie

The heraldic mark of the Melbourne City Council (MCC) from 1843 forged into civic signage and infrastructure.

Before the era of conceptual branding, logos tended to be more pictorial. Under the rather Skippy-esque kangaroo are symbolic depictions of the four most significant industries at the time – whaling, wool, cattle and maritime.

Fire branding

Some things are not as they seem. Featuring a rich visual language of embellished gold heraldry, firemarks suggest a civic, even aristocratic, authority. However, their intent is actually completely commercial.

Before the establishment of the Melbourne Fire Brigade (MFB), private insurance companies ran their own teams of firefighters and fire wagons. Firemarks were fixed to building façades, and were designed to identify the insurance company with whom the building owner had a policy. The inefficiency of having these 56 private fire brigades, along with their rather primitive methods of fire-fighting, eventually led to their unification under *The Fire Brigades Act* of 1890.

No longer working as policy-holder identifiers, the function of the firemarks shifted towards one of promotion. The grand design of these gleaming plates was well suited to this, typographically proclaiming all the traits one would wish of insurance – trustworthiness, strength and prestige. Perhaps the greatest comfort to Australians during this time was that they reinforced a strong connection to 'Mother England'. And so it was that insurance companies adopted names such as Imperial, Queen, Victoria and even Colonial, to make the association with the 'Mother Country' more explicit.

Once a common form of street signage, over time firemarks began disappearing from view as buildings were demolished or their façades refurbished. It is said that there are no firemarks remaining on buildings in Melbourne.[1]

OPPOSITE
Firemark for the Queen Insurance Company
(c. 1840–90)
pressed metal and paint
Image: State Library of Victoria Pictures Collection
H37389

RIGHT BOTTOM
An Anglo-centric heritage is reinforced on the firemarks both by the name, the graphic use of birds and other such traditionally English iconography (c. 1840–90)
pressed metal and paint
Image: State Library of Victoria Pictures Collection
H37389

RIGHT TOP
A grand example of (pre-MFB) private fire insurance signage in Fitzroy (2010)
Image: Lan Huang Courtesy of Letterbox

RIGHT TOP
Brigade signage alters from fire station to fire station (2011)
Image: Lan Huang Courtesy of Letterbox

P for post
T for telephones

So ever-present is typography in our lives that even when we look down at our feet we can't avoid interactions with letterforms. A simple stroll down any city street will have you noticing the imprinted initials of now redundant companies and authorities on metal plates and manhole covers – GFC, MMBW, MCCESB and, of course, PMG.[1]

With the abolition of the Post Master General's department (PMG) in 1975, the office's tasks were split across two new entities – Australia Post (to govern postal services) and Telecom (to oversee telecommunications). Not only did these organisations share the same establishment date, but a lesser-known fact is that their visual identities were crafted as a set by the same hand.

A specialist in corporate identity systems, the Dutch-born Pieter Huveneers was one among a wave of European émigrés who brought a new sense of internationalism to Australian design. An advocate of 'total design', Huveneers took a very broad and complete view of a business's identity systems. Speaking of the Australian context, he commented:

It is clear that the total design concept is not understood by many executives in industry today … It should be approached with a clear understanding on the part of the company of what corporate communication can contribute, and a designer must understand what the commercial processes can contribute to deliver the right identification to truly represent the nature and character of the industry now and for the next 10 to 15 years.[2]

The longevity of his corporate identity designs (many of which are still in use) stand as testimony to their ability to communicate. We can now observe, with the benefit of hindsight, that the 'total design' Huveneers espoused many decades ago is now a standard industry practice within the profession of branding.

The Australia Post logo is a monument to graphic simplicity. It cleverly positions the internationally recognised postal-horn device, a potent symbol of communication history, to form a letter P for Post. The circular element surrounding this represents movement, direction and global connection of people and communities. That the logo is still being used several decades after its design is testimony to its clarity and effectiveness. Its companion, the Telecom logo, also celebrated Huveneers' capacity for the power of visual abbreviation. Primarily typographic in nature, the central letter T for Telecom was designed to symbolise the semaphore system embracing the world, represented by a circle.

This identity came to an end some 18 years after its inception, when in 1993 Telecom began trading as Telstra. The identity for this new entity was created by Melbourne design firm

Flett, Henderson and Arnold (FHA), and involved the commissioning of a specific typeface to be used exclusively for Telstra.

And so it was that in 1999 the font family *Harmony*, designed by English type designer Jeremy Tankard, first emerged. It has since become a very distinctive and recognisable aspect of their corporate and public identity.

abcdefghijk
1234567890

TOP LEFT
Telecom identity
TOP RIGHT
Australia Post identity
were both developed in
1975 by Pieter Huveneers
(2009) *Image: Nick Kreisler*

ABOVE
Harmony typeface by
Jeremy Tankard (1998)

RIGHT
Lucy Wilson in the theatre
performance *Underwhere*
Hobart, Tasmania (2007)
Image: Peter Mathew

Lucy Wilson, the step-daughter of Pieter Huveneers, was so intrigued by the ubiquity of the Telecom logo, which lead to a fascination with the underworld, that she devised Underwhere, a theatrical performance depicting the urban underground's network of pipes and tunnels.

The White City

Modernity is widely thought to have first arrived in Melbourne at the same time as the staging of the 1956 Olympic Games. However, it may in fact have been a local confectioner who heralded in a social and industrial modernity many decades prior, his distinctive signage standing to this very day as a 'typeform of modernity'.[1]

The name MacRobertson's has been synonymous with confectionery products (including the creation of such popular items as the Cherry Ripe and Freddo Frog) since the company was first established in the late 1870s. However, its founder, Macpherson Robertson (1859–1945), was also a forward-thinking philanthropist, who put his name to many ventures in his lifetime, including an airline and a girl's high school, and donated money to fund Australian expeditions to the Antarctic.[2]

Macpherson Robertson's life reads as the classic 'rags-to-riches' story, as he steadily developed his business, first working in the bathroom of the family home, then eventually acquiring large parts of Fitzroy to make way for a cluster of factories.

This impressive set of 13 buildings, dubbed 'The White City', was regularly whitewashed (both inside and outside) and staffed by an army of factory workers (numbering 2500 by the 1930s), all dressed in white uniforms. He himself wore a white suit and it is said he had a carriage with two white ponies.[3]

The starkly efficient appearance of the factory, its progressive organisational structure and modern manufacturing processes, embodied the 'total designed system'. Each raw material, ingredient and process was controlled by the company, along with advertising and marketing.

Significant competition in the 1880s confectionery trade made Robertson realise that he would have to find a distinctive name as a point of difference in the marketplace. Using his full name Macpherson Robertson was the first and most obvious incarnation. But this was soon dropped as it was quite a mouthful to pronounce, besides taking up too much space. Eventually he ran the two names together, creating MacRobertson's – the name still used to this very day. Exhibiting his artistic flair he then created a distinctive signature, rich with flourishes, which then became the visual identity of both the man and the business. He even introduced a competition for schoolchildren, with a prize to the child who could best imitate the writing of his name.[4]

The image of the company and its philanthropic, progressive founder were so intrinsically interwoven that MacRobertson's literally stood for modernity. The MacRobertson name was a designed logotype, company symbol and trademark, as well as being the signature of the man.[5] In a structure that

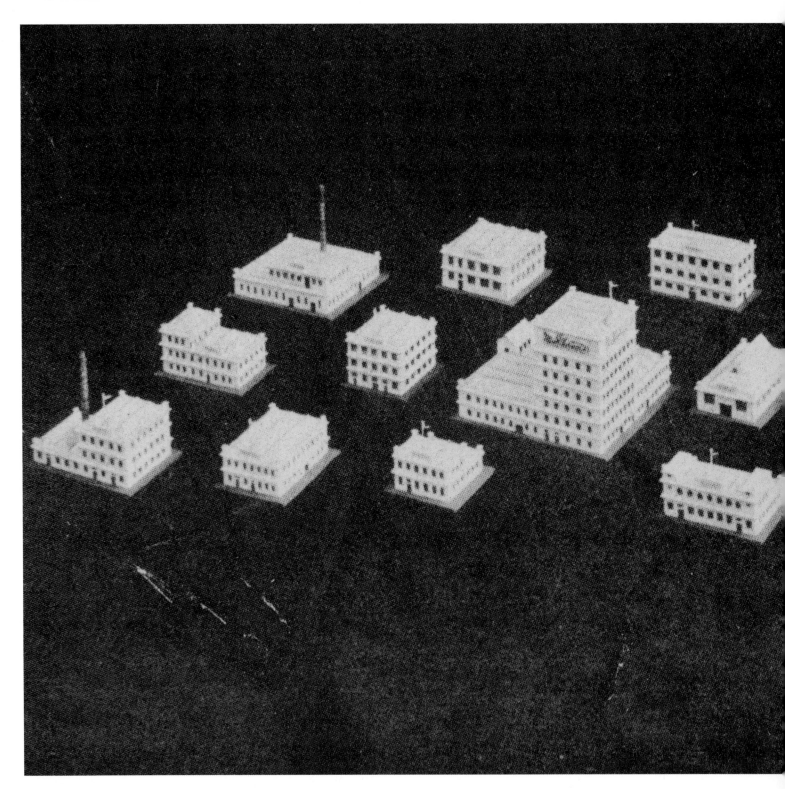

pre-empted contemporary branding strategies, the identity of the product and the producer were one.

The most dramatic presence of the MacRobertson's signature was a massive sign on the top of his Old Gold building. Standing some 36 metres high and just as wide, the huge illuminated sign contained some 1100 brilliant electric lamps and was described at the time as the 'largest and most attractive sign in the country'.[6] The June 1922 edition of the *Australasian Electrical Times* carried a vivid description:

> At either end of the sign is erected a rocket. In operation the rockets ascend and, bursting into a red flare, the streamers ignite the first letter of the word MacRobertson's. Immediately the word begins to write itself, when the whole word is entirely written lamp by lamp, the words Old Gold burst into view underneath in their typical colour. After a short pause the words are then obliterated gradually, as though being rubbed out, and so the action continues. Mr Tarrant, the chief electrician, designed, built and erected it. It can be seen as far east as Camberwell and Canterbury. It operates for five hours a night.[7]

In accordance with the MacRobertson's 'total design system' his sign was designed and constructed by the firm's electrical, plumbing and building staff.[8]

Photographed in his own 1921 memoirs, *A Young Man and a Nail Can*, the MacRobertson's sign is clearly one of the first in a continuum of spectacular illuminated signage. Pre-dating any of the better-known neon quartet (Pelaco, Nylex, Skipping Girl and Slade), its pyrotechnic design elements anticipate the Allen's Sweets sign erected more than 30 years later.

Although MacRobertson's moved their operations out to the outer-eastern suburb of Ringwood in 1966 and the founder's ubiquitous signature no longer lights up the Fitzroy night sky, much of the old confectionary factory network still exists. Many of these have since been converted into apartments across this now gentrified inner-city area. It is only the reward for the observant passer-by that the elaborate signature of MacRobertson's can still be seen tiled on top of many old factory façades of Fitzroy, indicating what was once the grand 'White City'.

ABOVE
Although most of 'The White City' has been converted into residential accommodation, the typographic presence of MacRobertson is still present today (2011) *Image: Lan Huang. Courtesy of Letterbox*

LEFT
A display of MacRobertson's 'White City' made entirely of sugar. From *Victoria in Pictures* (c.1938–45) published by The Argus and Australasian Ltd, Melbourne. *Image: State Library of Victoria La Trobe Collection*

ABOVE
The night-time illumination of the MacRobertson signage. Detail from *A Young Man and a Nail Can: An Industrial Romance* by MacRobertson's (firm) (1921) *Image: State Library of Victoria La Trobe Collection*

The King of Carlton

The tale of *The King of Carlton* is an extraordinary one, threading together the Second World War, the Olympic Games and the world of neon signage.

Italian cycling champion Nino Borsari (1911–96) rose to international prominence in the 1930s, his sporting prowess and showmanship making him immensely popular throughout Europe and the United States. During a trip to compete in Australia in 1939, hostilities broke out in Europe marking the beginning of the Second World War. Finding himself marooned in Sydney, Borsari sold his gold watch and bicycle, hitchhiked to Melbourne and found a job cycling on rollers at the Myer Department Store.

Although not interned like many of his fellow countrymen, he was warned against using his Italian name when opening up his own cycling shop in Carlton in 1941. He chose to ignore this, confident the locals would respect him enough to know that he had nothing to do with the War. His faith in public popularity proved right. Proudly named Borsari Emporium, the corner store operated for 50 years, eventually becoming known as the landmark 'Borsari's Corner'.

Today Borsari's sporting and cultural legacy takes the form of neon. The signage overlooking the corner of Grattan and Lygon Streets is one of the earliest neon signs still operating, having been erected in the late 1940s. The multi-coloured, illuminated neon depicts Borsari in his riding gear on his bike, along with the words 'Ex-Olympic Champion'. A set of Olympic rings sits above it on top of the roof. So highly respected was Borsari that he was even given the nickname of 'The King of Carlton'.

Borsari was outspoken in his pride for Australia and, more specifically, Melbourne. It has been speculated that his influence and connections within international sporting committees managed to sway support in favour of Melbourne's bid to host the 1956 Olympic Games, which it won by just one vote. The international exposure that came out of the 1956 Olympics changed Melbourne forever.

By 1967 so renowned was Borsari's Corner that when the Italian President Giuseppe Saragat was on a state visit to Australia, he chose it as the spot from which to deliver an important political speech televised in Italy.[1]

OPPOSITE
Borsari's Corner, Carlton (2011) *Image: Tim Fluence*

ABOVE
Nino Borsari (c.1936) *Image: Reproduced with permission of the CoAsIt Italian Historical Society*

The glowing park

An Italian flavour has been typographically immortalised in the strangest of places.

Any nightime passer-by on Brunswick's Albert Street could not help but notice a series of illuminated letterforms cast within a row of large, sculpted spheres. When read in sequence, the source of the park's inspiration is revealed – *Randazzo*.

Named after the Italian city of Randazzo, a sister-city to Melbourne at that time, this unique and striking typographic environment was designed on a new park site in 2002 by landscape architects Leanne O'Shea and Patrick Franklyn for the local Moreland City Council to address the lack of public parks and spaces for communal activity in the inner-city area.

Although at first glance the spheres in Randazzo Park appear to refer to the popular Italian game of boccé, commonly played in parks, O'Shea mentions other design influences:

> They [the spheres] reflect a common design strategy used in open spaces throughout Europe. We played with that idea to create an edge to the park whilst also providing lighting and signage all within the one element. As the site was originally a school our aim was also to be playful. [1]

This sense of playful community activity is further reinforced by the addition of a boccé park, children's playground and contemplative artworks elsewhere throughout the small park.

OPPOSITE
The typographic wonder of Randazzo Park (2011)
Image: Rhiannon Slatter

BELOW RIGHT AND LEFT
Randazzo Park in construction (2002)
Image: City of Moreland

Behind a well-known hotel neon lies the story of one of Australia's first billiard champions.

Poolside

Pick up a postcard of Melbourne
and invariably the view will show a
panorama of glistening skyscrapers
with the sweeping Yarra River in the
foreground. If the postcard happens to
depict Melbourne at night, a number of
illuminated signs will be visible, finely
tracing the city's southern-most edge
along Flinders Street. Among these, the
widely spaced titling of the Herald Sun
building is the most prominent, lending
the night sky an air of authority and
establishment. However just to the right
of this landmark there is a smaller but
nevertheless significant addition to the
neon profile of the city.

For Melbourne, the lighting up of the
squat in-line letters of the Lindrum Hotel
not only announce the presence of a
new generation of boutique hotels, but
also pay homage to the world-famous
billiards champion, Walter Lindrum.[1]

Born into a family of billiard champions,
Walter Albert Lindrum (1898–1960) was
given the initials W.A. by his father to
indicate the state of his birth, Western
Australia. Lindrum became one of
Australia's greatest sporting heroes,
with some 57 world records relating to
billiards to his name (many still standing).
He was even invited to exhibit his
billiards prowess to the King of England
and Royal family in Buckingham Palace
in 1931.

In 1973 the former Griffiths Tea
Building became a major focus of activity
as the major billiards and snooker-playing
establishment, the Lindrum Billiard
Centre.[2] Leased from News Limited by
Walter's niece, Dolly Lindrum, it not only
promoted the game of billiards, but also
reinforced the heritage of four generations
of billiards champions and snooker
players.

Following its closure in 1988 the owners
reclaimed the building, using it as a
publishing office. Three years after the
Herald Sun relocated its offices in 1995,
the building was redeveloped into the
luxury hotel that stands today.

The naming and prominent signage
of the building is not the only design
reference to Walter Lindrum. Countless
visitors to the Melbourne Cemetery
go to see his uniquely designed grave,
playfully fashioned as a billiard table,
complete with billiard balls and cues.

The caged kangaroo

Airline travel advertising is a celebration of personal freedom. Using a common visual language of birds, wings and open skies, airline companies conjure up dreams of comfortable and safe journeys to faraway and exotic destinations – and Qantas is no exception. The Qantas 'flying kangaroo' suggests an Australian dexterity and confidence in 'globe-hopping' anywhere around the world. However, behind the Qantas logo lies a lesser-known story of its designer, who lived a life that was anything but free.

The original Qantas symbol (created in 1944) was based on the kangaroo seen on the Australian one penny coin. It was first painted beneath the cockpit of a Qantas Liberator aircraft in Brisbane, after the company christened its Indian Ocean run the 'Kangaroo Service'.

Estonian-born architect and graphic designer, Gert Sellheim (1901–70) refined the original design in 1947, embellishing the iconic marsupial with wings, and in a nod to international flight, represented the kangaroo carrying a globe of the world at its feet. This design became the basis of subsequent Qantas logos used up to this very day.

However, only several years previously, during the Second World War, the German heritage of Sellheim's parents had caused the Australian government to consider him a Nazi sympathiser. Despite strong claims to abhor Hitler and his beliefs, this harsh judgement led to Sellheim's internment. It was only through family intervention that he was eventually released, on the undertaking that he perform work for the military. Ironically, after his period of incarceration Sellheim went on to design many posters for the Australian Tourism Authority, promoting Australia as an attractive holiday destination.

The Qantas logo has been revised several times since the original design. In 1958 the 'flying kangaroo' was placed in a circle and turned around to face the right. The acronym QANTAS (Queensland and Northern Territory Aerial Service) was added in a blocky sans serif upper-case italic font. In June 1984 Tony Lunn, of the Lunn Design Group, unveiled a new incarnation – this time with the wings removed and the kangaroo silhouette set in a triangle, representing the proportions of the airliner's tail fin, and featuring a much bolder typographic titling.

However, it was in 2007, when Qantas revised its logo once again, that the iconic brand re-entered public debate. The debate centred around the graphic representation of the kangaroo's leg, now more anatomically abstracted and stretched. Noted designer Ken Cato, who tweaked the Lunn design for the airline's 75th anniversary in 1995, described the 2007 'big-foot' version as 'ugly', instead preferring to see the possible return of the winged kangaroo design, something he said held certain mystical qualities. The response to the logo from the design and advertising industries was mostly negative, including a colourful description of the new logo as '… more pterodactyl than kangaroo'.[1]

1944
Unknown

1947
Gert Sellheim

1984
Lunn Design Group

2007
Hulsbosch
Communications

It's not every day you can eat a meal on a letter of the alphabet.
In Melbourne all it takes is a visit to a unique St Kilda landmark – Leo's Spaghetti Bar.

Pasta sans

The entire width of its Fitzroy Street restaurant façade is composed of three very large brick letters: L, E and O. Restaurant patrons sitting in the window seats may have no idea that they are actually eating their meals on a letterform. The three-part brickwork lettering correspondingly occupies the space where three small shop fronts once stood before they were destroyed in 1970 to make way for the current single-fronted façade.

Leo's was established by Leo Mastrototara, who longed to open a restaurant that offered a European alternative to the-then rather banal Australian diet, having lived in Australia since 1928 (including a period of internment during the Second World War).

So in 1956 he opened Leo's. Happily coinciding with Melbourne's hosting of the Olympic Games, the Spaghetti Bolognese and Cotoletta Milanese at Leo's quickly became a favourite among the visiting Italian team.

These days, both tourists and locals alike visit the Fitzroy Street institution, not only for the menu but also to see the unique typographic features of this architectural oddity.

Spaghetti type

Those Italians who were not interned during this period headed to the centres of Italian cultural activity situated in Bourke Street, the CBD, and Lygon Street, Carlton. The Society was only one in a group of Italian restaurants and cafés that had already emerged decades before this troubled period, and included Café Florentino (1928) and Café Latin (1930).

But it was the massive postwar influx of European immigrants and the exposure of Melbourne through the 1956 Olympic Games that really spurred on the growth of Italian restaurants and the signage that came with it – neon script.

The personalised nature of the restaurants, often named after their owners or their towns of origin, lent itself well to the most personalised form of typographic expression – the neon signature. Although not exclusive to Italian restaurants, flowing neon script is nevertheless a common feature of their joyous street presence and a wider celebratory cultural presence.

Historically, neon in Melbourne's CBD typically advertised entertainment rather than commerce. Signs such as Pellegrini's, Florentino, The Society and The Latin signalled the important and long-standing presence of the Italian community in the restaurant industry, particularly in the district below Parliament House in Bourke Street.[1]

In the case of Pellegrini's (1954), their neon signage runs for 10 metres down the side of the café. The laneway location of this neon is not about being shy, but instead reveals something of the history of the establishment, with the café once operating across several shop fronts in Crossley Lane. The neon was mounted on top of a large arrow pointing down the laneway (now removed).

The association between Italian restaurants and neon signage has led many to describe such neon tubing as 'spaghetti type'. For others it became a symbol of comfort, the familiarity of a 'home-cooked meal' and something that Melbourne holds very dear to its heart – decent coffee.

So strong was the anti-Italian sentiment during the years of the Second World War that The Italian Society restaurant decided to drop its reference to nationality, becoming simply 'The Society'.

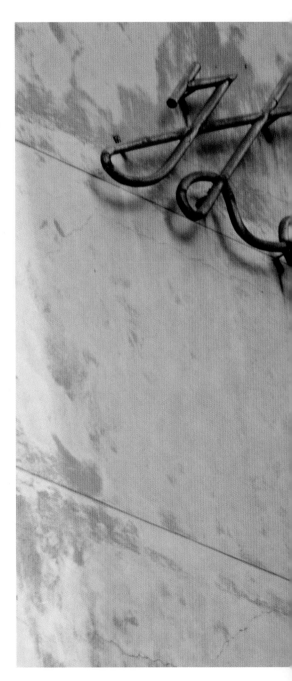

ABOVE
The gleaming metal
façade and signage of
The Graham Hotel was
a powerful symbol of
modernity (c. 1950–1970)
Peter Wille. Transparency
*Image: State Library of
Victoria Pictures Collection*
H91.244/4052

RIGHT
The Graham Hotel signage
is one of the most striking
yet least noticed signs in
Melbourne (2009)
Image: Nick Kriesler

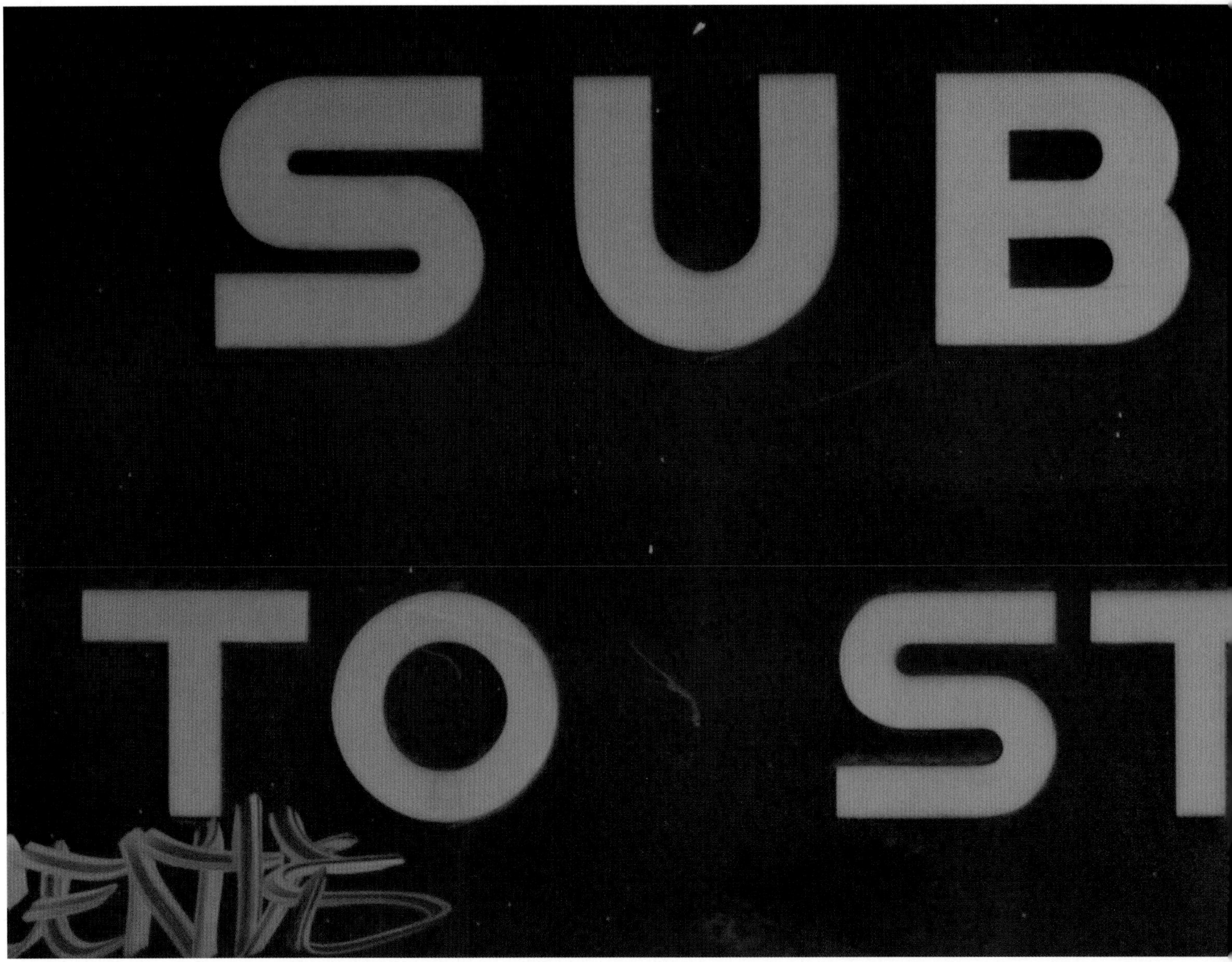
SUB
TO ST

Given the perpetual change of cities, completely preserved places are very rare.

Frozen in type

PAGES 96–97
The Campbell Arcade
entrance way sign
beckons commuters
downwards (2009)
Image: Nick Kriesler

OPPOSITE
One of the typographic
delights of Campbell
Arcade, the signage
stand for A Touch of Paris
(2009) *Image: Nick Kriesler*

PAGES 100–101
The voice of 1955;
telephone signage
in Campbell Arcade
(2009)
Image: Nick Kriesler

First proposed in 1926 but not constructed until 1955,[1] the Campbell Arcade (also known as Degraves Street Subway) was built just in time for the 1956 Melbourne Olympic Games to assist city commuters bypass crowds and readily access Melbourne's main railway station, Flinders Street Station. It features black granite columns and pink granite flooring and wall tiles, and was admired at the time for its neat shops and show windows. Once a bustling thoroughfare, the arcade suffered a dramatic drop in patronage after the opening of the city train loop in the early 1980s. After decades of neglect, the arcade now offers a unique glimpse of what Melbourne looked like over 50 years ago.

This largely original mid-twentieth-century design environment also features many frozen typographic details. The elegantly curved, three-dimensional signs gesture towards an alcove where public telephone boxes once stood, a reminder of an era before the advent of mobile phones. As well as offering convenient train commuter access, Campbell Arcade was positioned directly underneath the Mutual Store, once Melbourne's largest department store.

Remnants of signage gesturing to the store can still be seen curved around the salmon-coloured, tiled walls, pointing absurdly to a sealed blank wall. When it was first built the arcade's large inset glass cases, running along half its length, displayed Mutual Store products as it led customers up a stairway into the magnificent grand emporium.

These cases now have a new purpose – exhibiting art to the sometimes bewildered, sometimes receptive, flow of rail commuters who use this subterranean short-cut.

With the decommissioning of the arcade railway booking office in the 1990s much of the hand-painted copper-plate lettering was lost. More recent and equally appealing typographic expression can be found in the resourceful signage of the various small independent boutiques that now line the arcade.

The sign announcing a price rise from $12 to $15 at the hairdresser, A Touch of Paris, is indicated in the most direct way possible – by simply turning the numeral upside down.

The story of the 'lost' bowling alley

For many years people have speculated that there is an old abandoned underground bowling alley accessible through the Campbell Arcade. Council records indicate that a bowling alley was indeed built in the basement of the Mutual Store in 1964 for a sum of £10,000.

Creating leisure experiences in city stores was common at a time when the appeal and convenience of suburban shopping centres was starting to draw shoppers away from the city centre. Sadly, after only a few years the bowling alley was closed down and has since faded into city folklore.

OPPOSITE
A passport photography
shopfront in Campbell
Arcade (1991)
Image: Warren Kirk

ABOVE
Typographic traces of
exits long since sealed up.
This one gestures to the
Mutual Store that once
sat above on Flinders
Street (2009)
Image: Nick Kriesler

RIGHT
The train ticketing office
windows, removed in the
late 1990s (1994)
Image: Author

Commonly held wisdom says that fast cars call for fast signage – big and bold letterforms to match the accelerated speed of car culture. However, one large sign in Melbourne's southern suburbs was apparently a bit *too* fast for the traffic.

The changing lights at the changing lights

The iconic Victoria Bitter skysign that sits on top of the Elsternwick Hotel was installed in 1951 to capitalise on its position overlooking a busy intersection on a main north and south thoroughfare. It was a time when more and more people were starting to use cars as their main means of transport. Heavier traffic meant a longer wait at the intersection for the lights to change, and that meant a growing captive audience to view the sign.

The original Victoria Bitter sign featured a set of white chaser globes that offered the commuter an eye-catching, animated spectacle of light and colour. However, it was not long before the road traffic authorities and the local council began to express concern that this new and exciting roadside display was distracting drivers from concentrating on the road. The number of people driving, combined with the potentially hazardous distraction of flickering neon at a major intersection was enough to persuade the authorities to act. As one of the veterans of the Melbourne neon industry, Nevin Phillips recalls: 'At one stage we couldn't use green on a neon sign near intersections, because you'd see the sign before you would see the lights'.[1] So it was agreed that the signage could stay but only in a non-animated form.[2] The globes were removed and replaced with a static neon frame.

The Victoria Bitter skysign is unique in many ways, as it advertises a product that still exists much as it did when the sign was first constructed, and its usage rights still continue. It is also possibly the second oldest large neon moving skysign remaining in use featuring movement (after the famed PELACO sign in Richmond).

Now reduced to its static form, the Elsternwick Hotel skysign joins the other two significant Victoria Bitter signs on the same thoroughfare. The largest of all three sits on top of Richmond's Barrett Burston silos, alongside the renowned Nylex sign. A third sign looms large over the intersection of Toorak and Punt Roads, provocatively extolling the virtues of alcohol consumption to its neighbour across the road, the local Anglican church.

Speed reading

For centuries shop signage was designed to attract the slow-moving passer-by, displayed at eye level and viewed at a casual walking pace. Signs were made to human scale. In the mid-twentieth century something completely changed this relationship – the automobile.

PAGES 108–109
The Oakleigh Motel (1959)
*Image: National Archives
of Australia*

BELOW
Postcard of the Oakleigh
Motel (c.1957)
Rose Stereograph Co.
Glass negative
*Image: State Library of
Victoria Pictures Collection*
H32492/8764

OPPOSITE
*Official Guide: XVIth
Olympiad, Melbourne
1956*, showing the
marathon route turning
at Oakleigh, the exact site
of the proposed motel.
*Image: City of Melbourne
Art and Heritage Collection
Photograph: Louis Porter*

THE ROSE SERIES P. 13961   OAKLEIGH MOTEL, 10 MILES FROM THE HEART OF MELBOURNE, VIC.
COPYRIGHT.

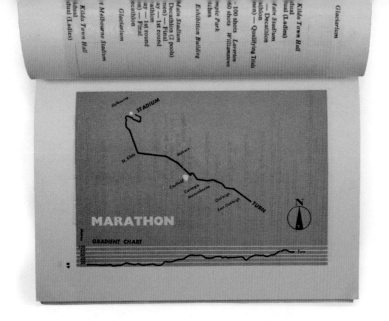

Many saw this development as 'a rude assault on the conventional boundary between neighbourhood and street – neon company logos, massive advertising hoardings and catchy slogans all competed to catch the eye of the speeding motorist'.[1]

However, others saw it as a great opportunity, and so this new mobility was serviced by a rash of new suburban shopping centres, drive-in movie theatres, freeways and motels.

The first motel to be built in Victoria, the Oakleigh Motel, was noted as much for its typographic signage as for the popular offerings it boasted, such as 'Your car in your bedroom' (meaning that guests could park their cars at their door for easy access).

The motel's graphic immediacy was unashamedly American in influence – feeding scorn from architectural critics such as Robin Boyd, who derided this new colourful and often garish form as 'Austerica'.[2]

The motel was the brainchild of Cyril J. Lewis, 'formerly well known in the car-selling game', who had toured throughout the United States, inspecting motels and gathering inspiration for building one in Melbourne to coincide with the 1956 Olympic Games.

Unfortunately, delays in construction meant that the motel was not finished until 1957. This was a great disappointment for the entrepreneurial Lewis as he could not capitalise on its very deliberately chosen geographic location – the exact spot where the long distance Olympic marathon runners turned around to return to the city. Such public exposure would clearly have been great publicity for this statement of international modernity. After all, it was signage, especially illuminated lettering, that was so closely associated with modern design in postwar architecture, allowing shops and businesses to boldly advertise their location and function, day and night.

In the case of the Oakleigh Motel, the building itself was almost dwarfed by its broad and brazen billboard-style signage. Above the office area was a sloping panel with the words 'OAKLEIGH MOTEL' emblazoned in red letters, set forward off the wall and illuminated at night. After the initial construction, a further large rectangular neon sign was added to the roof with the word 'MOTEL' and an arrow featuring the word 'OAKLEIGH' down one side.

Despite its unique typographic offerings and its status as Victoria's first motel, a battle waged for many years over whether to protect the Oakleigh Motel or demolish it. In defending the motel, the National Trust, stated:

The Oakleigh Motel is the earliest, most famous, and remarkably intact example in Victoria of the new 'Motel Hotel' concept. It is also an important example of the colourful, eye-catching roadside architecture typical of the 1950s.[3]

However, such significance provided no protection and in 2010 the Oakleigh Motel was stripped of much of its original features to be developed into townhouses. Currently only part of the façade remains, giving the viewer little insight into its earlier modern splendour.

If there was ever a typographic shrine to celebrate automobile culture it would have to be the suburban drive-in. It was also the birthplace of one of Australia's first totally integrated visual identity systems – a little stick figure called *Skyline Sam*, who has now vanished from history.

Simple Sam

For the patrons of the drive-in, a sense of event is paramount. For the drive-in operators this means offering a visual spectacular of dramatic light, colour and movement, and that's before the film screening starts. One of the first operators to pioneer the importance of the 'visual entrée' was the drive-in chain Skyline. Towering high above the white rock-lined drive-in entrances stood the immediately recognisable, glowing Skyline sign, its brightly illuminated letterforms standing some 1.5 metres high. Below it, closer to eye level, was an illuminated backboard listing the films on offer.

Like the Oakleigh Motel, initial inspiration for drive-ins came from observing postwar social trends throughout the United States. One of the first to see this phenomena and bring it to Australia was George Griffith Jnr. Despite being Hoyts' southern divisional manager, Griffith Jnr could not persuade his superiors to see the potential of this new entertainment medium in Australia. And so he began his own operation, Skyline, opening up Australia's first drive-in in Burwood, Melbourne, in 1954. Its immediate success spawned a national chain of drive-ins.

The ability of Skyline to create what may now be described as an 'integrated customer experience' was unique, and with this came one of Australia's first home-grown graphic identities – Skyline Sam. The stick-figure simplicity of Skyline Sam evolved from the early use of the character in a 60-second animated film instructing patrons how to attach and operate the speaker systems at the drive-in. He then appeared in illuminated form alongside the ticket box welcoming patrons, on café lamp fittings, as well as in general press advertising, reinforcing his iconic status.

Being a simple stick figure, he was easily modified to suit different themes. A 1957 press advertisement for a drive-in 'Ranch Night' saw Skyline Sam wearing appropriate cowboy attire, while the screenings during the 1956 Olympic period had him curiously appearing in Negro 'blackface' and top hat.

His stick-figure form also made it easier and more affordable to fabricate as signage. As drive-in historian David Kilderry explains, 'By himself he means nothing. He doesn't tie to movies at all, but Skyline was so good with having him

OPPOSITE
A digital reconstruction of the 60-second instructional film featuring Skyline Sam who helped drive-in patrons connect the speakers to their cars
Image: Lan Huang Courtesy of Letterbox

LEFT
Advertisement featuring Skyline Sam dressed up for a theme night in *The Herald* (13 March 1957, p. 32)

ABOVE
Advertisement from *The Sun* (23 Nov 1956, p. 44) *Both images: State Library of Victoria Newspapers Collection*

associated with everything to do with the drive-in that when people saw him they thought drive-ins'.[1]

So popular were the early drive-ins that they would cause nightly traffic jams through neighbouring suburban streets, creating great inconvenience for local residents. The Burwood Skyline Drive-in found a lateral solution to this, and wired drive-in speakers into the homes that backed onto their property so that they could at least enjoy listening to the movies they could see from their back windows.

Although widespread during the 1950s, by the time of the 1963 rebranding of Skyline (now owned by Hoyts), Skyline Sam had vanished from the drive-ins. Virtually nothing exists of this early period of entertainment branding, and as a result he has slipped away from public memory and design history.

The steady demise of the drive-in, primarily because of the widespread household adoption of television along with other changing social trends, has left only three drive-ins still operating today out of the 60 or more that once existed. The heritage classification of one of these, the Dromana drive-in on the Mornington Peninsula, includes the distinctive neon script signage positioned on the rear of Screen One. Spelling out the original name of the 1961 drive-In, 'Peninsula', the illuminated signage faces the bayside township of Dromana, overlooking a recently constructed freeway, and is considered by locals to be a striking and culturally important beacon indicating arrival to the Peninsula area.

In 1990 the glittering Coca-Cola sign above St Kilda Junction lit up in an unexpected way when it caught fire. This flaming centrepeice of the intersection was eventually extinguished, followed by a speedy overnight repair by a small army of maintenance men. Within 24 hours the integrity of the Coca-Cola corporate image had been restored to a bemused viewing public.

At the intersection of topography and typography

Signage is pragmatic; it is placed at locations that offer maximum exposure and sustained viewing. What better place than a huge intersection to capture the attention of drivers as they drive past or sit waiting for the lights to change. However, any major change to the direction, location or width of roadways (urban topography) brings with it a corresponding shift in the form and position of signage (urban typography). Perhaps the most striking example of this was the redesign of Melbourne's most renowned and largest intersection, the famed St Kilda Road Junction.

Glowing neon has long been the 'preferred medium of choice' for advertisers using St Kilda Junction, giving the intersection a lively ambience of colour and movement. In the heyday of motoring, Ethyl, of Atlantic Ethyl fame, posed with her hair blowing in the breeze as she advertised the Atlantic brand of petroleum, while across from her was the Shell Petroleum's monumental Tumbling Dice (1958). This spectacular sequence would begin with the illuminated statement 'Don't Gamble', followed by a set of dice famously tumbling down a 17-metre drop with the outcome impossible to predict.[1] The finishing statement 'Use Shell' then completed the circuit.

Not only did the Tumbling Dice prove to be free public entertainment, it also provided a chance for those who were inclined to place a wager.[2] Even the *Shell Journal* from April 1958 speculated on its usage: 'It will be interesting to see whether it becomes a kind of unofficial lottery in the area around St Kilda Junction.'[3]

Prospective betters had to be fast as the combination of numbers was controlled by a slipping switch, which created a new sequence every 10 seconds. As Nevin Phillips from Delta Neon recalls,

The dice tumbled and you couldn't cheat with it ... the bookmakers used to stand on the opposite corner with a crowd of blokes all trying their luck. Eventually they had to ban it because it was being used so much for gambling.[4]

And so down came 460 metres of coloured neon, 40 transformers and 20 special switches. It seems that despite the brightly advertising message not to gamble, it proved too much of a temptation for many.

Unsurprisingly at this time, most of the illuminated junction signage promoted products relating to motoring – 'Esso for Happy Motoring' and 'Dunlop Tyres and Batteries', among many others. The use of neon was viewed by many in the motor trade as a new form of 'scientific' advertising, well suited to the notions of progress and speed portrayed by the modern streamlined motor vehicle.

The complete reconfiguration of St Kilda Junction in 1963 required not only the removal of many trees (to the dismay and public protest of many), but also the demolition of many houses and buildings, together with their glowing crowns of neon.[5]

Modern-day St Kilda Junction continues to feature a wide array of large-scale advertising signs. And as traffic steadily increases along this very busy thoroughfare, the advertising worth and exposure of these sites also increases.

Spinning a tale of signage

There was a one hundred foot (30-metre) tower outside the Ford factory in Broadmeadows. Don Fraser and I had to put this revolving Falcon on the top of this tower with [Reg] Ansett's helicopter. So we're both on the top of this bloody great tower, that when you climbed up in it, if you shook it, it kept going for about five minutes before it stopped. We put this revolving Falcon, a great big thing, lowering it down. It was beaut. But the moment the air from the [helicopter] blades hit the top of the tower, the falcon started to spin erratically. Nearly knocked us off. We both flattened ourselves and crawled down inside the tower. Back then Don Fraser was a bit of a madman and eventually he grabbed hold of [the car] and managed to get it down and bolt it in. It was all a bit of a stupid thing to do.

Nevin Phillips | DELTA NEON

Beacon of the west

It's large, pointy and bright.
It's the Apex Belting sign,
lighting the way to the west.

The multi-coloured neon titling for Apex Belting is framed by a sequence of chaser globes mounted on a shape pointed at the top to make an apex. Although significantly smaller in stature than the better known 'neon quartet' of Richmond,[1] the Apex Belting sign lays claim to being the longest continuously operational neon sign in Melbourne, possibly Australia.[2] As the date of its original installation was not documented (it is anecdotally estimated to have been around 1940), this celebrated claim is still open to conjecture.

Regardless of these technicalities, the Apex Belting signage is a treasured landmark in an area renowned for its manufacturing heritage. 'Belting' refers to the company's stock and trade – the manufacture of conveyor belting for mining and industrial purposes. The popularity of the sign among the public became immediately apparent when it was being taken down for repairs in July 2002. The National Marketing Manager of Apex Fenner, Graeme Vickory recalls, 'They all wanted to know where it had gone and when it would be back.'[3]

Local Maribyrnong mayor, Mill Horrocks, reflected on boyhood memories of the sign as he travelled from Geelong to Melbourne: 'It meant we were just about there, or 100 yards from the footy'.[4]

In the process of restoring the sign, workers cleaned out many bird nests, as well as discovering two bullet holes.[5]

OPPOSITE AND OVERLEAF
The Apex Belting sign,
a glistening landmark
of the western suburbs
(2011) *Images: Jesse Marlow*

All lit up and nowhere to go.

The story of the Allen's Sweets sign.

Signage is a passionate topic. Some people love it while others loathe it. Aware of this public division, the Outdoor Advertising Association of Australia (OAAA) commissioned a study into community attitudes to outdoor signage in 1975. The study stated:

[I]t seems that for most people ... illuminated signs ... contribute to the character of the city. Character itself is a complex thing. It is partly the ability of a city to 'feel right'; to provide the functions that many expect of a city – a lively commercial scene, brightness and colour, calm areas, impressive buildings, people actively pursuing their own business. Partly it is a symbolic thing. It relates to special features of a city, which to some extent become identified with that city and ... in mental shorthand form, use them to think and feel emotionally about those cities.[1]

Eight years later these very findings were used to try to stop the demolition of one of the most significant neon signs in Melbourne's history – the Allen's Sweets sign.

With its prominent riverside position, multi-layered complexity and colourful animation, the Allen's 'skyline spectacular' made it one of the most charming and memorable signs of its kind. The proposal to save the sign ultimately failed and in 1987 the structure came crashing down.

With it went a long history of riverside neon signage that once flickered its way along the Yarra from the rooftops of buildings along the river front to Flinders Street Station and beyond.

Other than a rigidly enforced 'black-out' of neon signage during the Second World War, Melbourne's riverside area, today known as Southbank, was ablaze with an assortment of bright typographic neon signs for many decades.

CLAUDE
NEON

FAMILY SIZE

OPPOSITE
The massive typography
of the Allen's sign (1986)
Erica Downward
*Images: State Library
of Victoria Pictures Collection*
H2011.71/152

THIS PAGE
The Allen's confectionery
factory on what is now
Southbank. *Image:
Courtesy of Claude Neon*

TOP RIGHT, TOP LEFT
AND BOTTOM LEFT
Allen's Sweets sign at
night, South Melbourne
(c.1986)
Robert Colvin
photographs, gelatin
silver, selenium toned
*Images: State Library
of Victoria Pictures
Collection* H91.212/2
H91.212/3, H91.212/1

BOTTOM RIGHT
The Allen's factory (1986)
Erica Downward
*Image: State Library
of Victoria Pictures Collection*
H2011.71/127

OPPOSITE
The Allen's sign sequence
reproduced in Erica
Downward's *The Sweetest
of Them All: The history of
the Allen's neon sign* (1987)
*Images: State Library
of Victoria La Trobe
Collection, Courtesy of
Claude neon*

(a) <u>Allen's Sweets Base Message</u>

(b) <u>Sky Rocket Overlay</u>

(c) <u>Kool Mints Overlay</u>

(d) <u>Anticol Overlay</u>

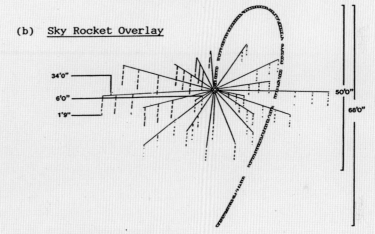

11

The Allen's sign was, in fact, a relative latecomer, sitting on top of what was once the Holden auto factory and fixed to the very framework that once announced the release of the first Australian-made car, the Holden FX, in 1948.[2]

The many forms of Allen's

The Allen's sign had three incarnations, each becoming more complex than the last. The first Allen's sign (1955–63) featured a three-tiered message – the distinctive italic Allen's logo on the top, the words 'Irish Moss' below this and the words 'Gum Jubes' at the bottom. Over the top of this base structure appeared the words 'Q.T. Fruit Drops'. This display was sequenced in such a way that the different messages flashed every six seconds or so.

The second version of the Allen's sign (1963–69) utilised some of the original elements and built upon them. This time the Allen's logo was contained within a lolly wrapper shape, underneath which were the words 'Your Flavorite Sweets'. The overlay was far more illustrative, initially featuring 'Cheers Fruit Drops', with a packet and two lozenges in neon, which was later changed to 'Anticol', with a packet, two lozenges and the words 'Cough Drops'.

However, it was at the suggestion of its manufacturers, Claude Neon, that a third (1969–87) Allen's sign was built, capitalising on updated technology to create eye-catching animation and greater illumination, even in the daytime.

To achieve this, four main illumination sequences were designed: the Allen's Sweets logo, the word 'Sweets' and the lolly wrapper shape; the renowned 'sky-rocket' overlay, whereby 'a rocket of yellow lights soars in an arc over the outline of an Allen's twist-wrapped toffee. It bursts into multi-coloured rays in the centre of the sign, and then fades into animated sparks'[3]; the 'Cool Cool' overlay, featuring the words 'Cool Cool' ('There is snow on the cool so you knew how cool it was'[4]) next to the Kool Mints logo; and finally, the Anticol overlay, consisting of an open Anticol packet with two lozenges tumbling out one after the other, and the words 'Cough Drops' underneath.

For nearly 20 years the nightly throng of pedestrians along Princes Bridge would marvel at these bright and colourful animated sequences.

As one of Claude Neon's employees said of the sign at the time of its installation:

[It] will create an effect and impact unique to Melbourne. This highly animated introduction to each of the product messages creates an effect on viewers of a dramatic fascinating ever-changing panorama.[5]

Another remarked:

'this is not just advertising, this is a landmark'.[6]

When it was discovered that the development plans for the 'Riverside quay' did not include the Allen's sign, a concerted campaign was mounted to relocate it.

Involving the developer Costain, Claude Neon (who owned the sign), Allen's Sweets (who owned the building) and the Ministry for Planning and Environment (who wanted the sign preserved),[7] a working party was established to propose several possible sites.

The most viable proposal at the time was for the sign to be relocated on top of RMIT (Royal Melbourne Institute of Technology) in Swanston Street. Jim Sinatra, then head of the RMIT Landscape Architecture Department, argued that the sign 'is as much a part of the urban heritage as Skipping Girl', and would contribute to a campus that 'lacks pizzazz and identity, and needs something special to give it colour and life'.[8]

Likewise, Allen's Sweets, which was believed to have offered $250,000 to cover the costs of its relocation, thought that the stark façade of the institute 'might benefit from a bit of light'.[9] But it was the very public exposure of the new site that met with opposition from the Melbourne City Council, whose '... policy has been in the past to restrict signage on educational and civic buildings to non-commercial advertisements'.[10] Sinatra continued to argue: 'It's a matter of seeing how much support is received from the staff and students. We could not do something like this without a high degree of public support.'[11]

Despite the numerous newspaper articles bemoaning its impending demise, the Allen's Sweets sign relocation proposal never found favour with the RMIT Council and was not adopted.

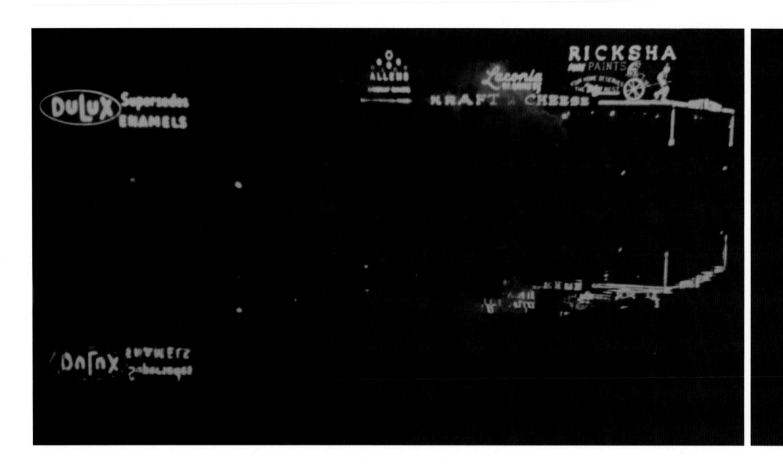

ABOVE
The reflections of the
original Allen's sign with
its neon contemporaries
– Dulux Paints, Laconia
Woollen Mills, Kraft
Cheese and Rickshaw
Paints. Not one of these
signs remains in existence.
*Image: City of Melbourne
Art and Heritage Collection*

Renowned Melbourne playwright Barry
Dickins reflected on the uncertain fate
of the Allen's sign:

*Like a lot of romantic people I've often
stood on the embankment near Flinders
Street Station and watched all the lollies
change. It's like a big red heart with green
tears. They can stick it on top of my place
if they like.*[12]

That would be hard to do with a sign
that measures some 30 metres across
and 22 metres tall!

The preservation debate around the
Allen's sign typifies the complexity of
custody – the neon company owns the
sign, the advertiser leases it, the sites are
owned by developers and while many
arms of government see merit in their
preservation, they are often hamstrung

The bitter sweet life of the Allen's 'skyline spectacular'

1930s
Illuminated signage established across the Yarra River on the southern side.

1940–45
All neon signage 'blacked out' during the Second World War.

1948
Holden signage erected announcing the Holden FX.

1955
Original version of the Allen's sign erected on top of the old Holden factory building, in the area now known as Southbank.

1963
Second incarnation of Allen's sign installed.

1969
Third (and final) version of the Allen's sign created, incorporating more complex and detailed animation sequences.

1987
The Allen's sign is removed from the Melbourne skyline and never seen again.

1990 – current day
Rumours persist that the dismantled Allen's sign has been stored in a warehouse, feeding speculation of its possible return.

by bureaucratic processes and politics. Bill Isaacs, National Sales Manager at Claude Neon, summed up the sentiment: 'Everybody wants it to remain, but they've got their hands stuck in their pockets. No one wants to pay for it.'

And then there are the ever-shifting definitions of what is historical and what is not. Ray Tonkin of the Historic Buildings Council said of the Allen's sign: 'It's not historical in the normal sense of the word although it is old for a neon sign. We're more interested in its value as public art, its aesthetic significance.'[13]

The folklore of Allen's

Even years after vanishing from the Melbourne skyline, rumours abounded as to the actual whereabouts of the Allen's sign with it considerable metal framework and masses of complex neon tubing. The most common theory was that it had been salvaged intact by Claude Neon and was stored in a remote warehouse somewhere. The truth is less hopeful. 'Nope, it all came crashing down in a thousand pieces', said Rick Charylo, who witnessed the final moments of the Allen's sign as his company demolished the factory site.[14] Charylo explained that the demolition company had two options – carefully take it apart and store it away for years until somebody wanted it or just demolish it. They decided on the latter option.

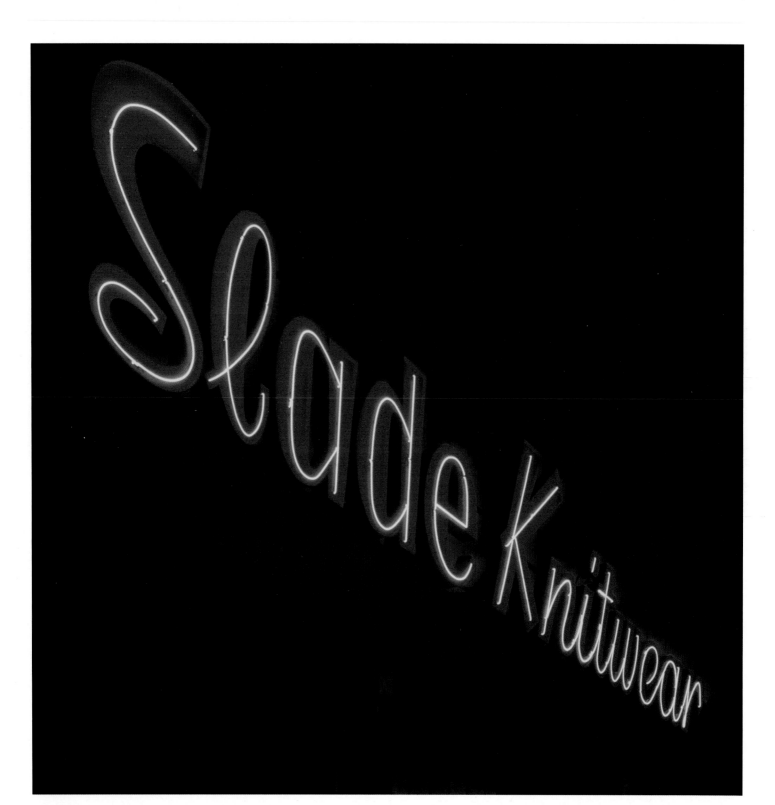

Written by the hand of a giant

'The letters are huge, vastly expanded things – it looks like someone has hand-written the Slade sign and blown it up to enormous [size]. It has this curious juxtaposition of scale ... as if written by the hand of a giant.'[1]

Originally designed to be positioned on Punt Road, one of Melbourne's main arterial roads, the visual dominance of the Slade Knitwear sign is magnified by its eventual position overlooking a narrow back street in Cremorne, a former industrial zone of Richmond.

The sheer dimensions of the sign are indeed impressive – spanning some 31 metres in width, the capital letters (S&K) stand 4.5 metres tall, the lowercase letters 2.3 metres tall. Like the other members of the 'neon quartet' (comprising the Skipping Girl, Nylex, Pelaco and Slade signs), there have been pitched battles between those who wish to see the Slade Knitwear sign disappear and those who wish to continue enjoying the alluring and seductive qualities of its bright red neon.

We have a wonderful view of the north bank of South Yarra, and all the trees and nice apartments that surround it, but the best view is of the Slade Knitwear sign. The glow of the neon tends to bend around corners and bounce off the rooftops, and it was pretty much a definitive consideration for us moving into the area. There's something seductive about neon signs. That seduction has been lost in streetscape signage such as billboards. But there's something very alluring about neon.[2]

In a submission to Heritage Victoria to support a protection order, the local activist group RING (Residents in a Neon Glow) specifically referred to the nature of the sign's typography as one of the reasons for its ongoing preservation. They stated that, unlike the more common sans serif titling used on the Pelaco sign, the cursive script used on the Slade Knitwear sign was not in widespread use.[3] Conversely, it was then argued that because the sign was erected in 1970, the font style was not an authentic relic of the period it sought to represent (the 1930s and 1940s). Never before had such a public debate centred around the finer points of typographic history.

Australian Neon argued that the sign had to come down (to be replaced by a backlit billboard) in the interest of public safety: 'Our biggest concern is that if one of the letters were to come down, it would be absolutely shocking if someone was killed or injured ...'[4] However, this argument was not unanimously supported by all of the engineering inspection reports.

Local residents continued to be active in the fight to save the signage. In 1995 architect Craig Rossetti and photographer Tim Griffith produced a special set of Christmas cards, which were then sent out to local councillors in an effort to influence their viewpoints. These cards featured atmospheric images of a Christmas tree set among the Cremorne area with the all-important Slade Knitwear sign warmly glowing in the background.[5]

Recognising the significance of the signage, the Council decided not to issue a permit to replace it. Although protection of the Slade Knitwear site was finally granted in 2001, the ongoing cost of electricity remains the main point of debate.

The sign currently remains in place but does not light up. Perhaps one night the streets of Cremorne will once again be bathed in the warm red glow of this typographic spectacular.

PREVIOUS PAGES
AND OPPOSITE
The warm glow of the
Slade Knitwear sign
(1995)
Image: Tim Griffith

Get shirty

It flickered away in the background of the classic post-punk film *Dogs in Space,* and its threatened removal inspired widespread public protest. It is the Pelaco sign.

Perhaps now better known than the shirts the company produces, the Pelaco skysign that sits on top of Richmond Hill is one of the oldest, largest and most recognisable typographic landmarks in Melbourne today.

As the August 1939 issue of the Pelaco staff newsletter, *Pelacograms*, declared: 'Yes, we're getting a new neon sign soon, fourteen foot letters and double sided on the very pinnacle of the roof. All Melbourne will know where we "hang out"'.

Installed by Claude Neon in 1939, the Pelaco sign stands 4.3 metres high and is made up of 15 tonnes of steel and 250 metres of light tubing. It was designed to create a dynamic lighting sequence of globes and neon tubing to give the

illusion of movement. Each letter was illuminated individually in sequence in red neon. After the 'O' the entire word went off and on again. Then the word and frame went off and the sequence was repeated.

As one of the city's first neon signs, the Pelaco signage is indicative of the innovative, efficient and socially progressive industrial culture that existed at the shirt manufacturer.

Even the name itself tells a story of its beginnings – Pelaco is a composite of the first two letters in the surnames of its founders, James Kerr <u>Pe</u>arson and James Lindsay <u>La</u>w, and its status as a <u>Co</u>mpany.

Appearing in no fewer than ten scenes in the classic post-punk film *Dogs in Space* (1987), the Pelaco sign is a treasured cultural asset. Now classified by the National Trust, it even once featured on the front cover of *Sunday Life* magazine,[1] with the headline 'Hands off! The bits of Melbourne we're not allowed to touch'.

It is widely recognised as symbolising not only the history of Pelaco but the heyday of the once flourishing Australian textile trade. Although the Pelaco company no longer operates from the Goodwood Street site, the broad community support for the sign's preservation (known as the 'Get shirty' campaign) led to its publically celebrated re-lighting on 6 October 1997.

PREVIOUS PAGES
The massive span of
the Pelaco sign (1995)
Image: Author

LEFT AND RIGHT
Just two of the ten
appearances the Pelaco
sign made during the
classic post-punk film
Dogs in Space (1987)
*Image: Courtesy of
Richard Lowenstein*

6.38 It is said that during the month of May in 2006 Melbourne workers experienced more late morning starts than usual. The reason was simple. The Nylex clock that overlooks Punt Road was frozen at 6.38 due to a power surge.

The clock is just one part of a much-loved sign that has become one of the most distinctive and visible typographic landmarks of Melbourne. Imported from Chicago and installed in 1967, the Nylex sign's position on top of the towering Barrett Burston silos makes it visible right across eastern Melbourne.

Nylex claimed it would be seen by thousands of commuters as they drove to and from work along several of the city's main arterial roads, and thousands more would see it from trains travelling to the eastern and southern suburbs.[1]

This recognition and longevity have etched it deep into the psyche of Melbournians, who use the clock and its accompanying temperature gauge to see not only how late they are, but whether it is hot or cold. Its social value is immense. When the Nylex clock was restarted in August 2004, after being out of action for 14 months, the event was covered as a live broadcast by a leading commercial radio station. It has also been immortalised in the song 'Leaps and Bounds' by Paul Kelly, which features the line '... and way up high on the clock on the silo says 11 degrees ...'

The Nylex sign visible today is in fact its second incarnation. The original version featured the top line (spelling out NYLEX) in the same expanded slab serif typeface (the same style as the current line spelling PLASTICS). This was then changed in 1970 to Helvetica, a font style popular at the time. The sign consists of the words NYLEX PLASTICS and is crowned by an LED thermometer display/clock.

The illuminated word NYLEX is formed by single rows of lightbulbs within metal troughs. The slab serif word PLASTICS is outlined in neon tubing. A second layer is then achieved by a further overlaid set of neon tube lettering spelling EVERY TIME.

The grandness of the Nylex signage befitted the scale and innovation of the company it advertised. After all, it was the first plastics company established in Australia (1927), as well as the largest. The Nylex sign is a rare surviving example of a once common form of 'skysign' that emerged in the 1930s and reached its height of popularity in the 1960s – the very era of the Nylex installation. So high was the cost of its installation ($1000 in 1967) that the new sign was publicly nicknamed 'Derham's folly', referring to Peter Derham, son of founder John Derham, who was general manager at the time.[2]

What started as a folly may well have become a disaster. Over the years the wheat dust from the silos below had the effect of eating away many of the metal fixings, possibly making the sign a public danger.[3]

Now that the Nylex signage has the protection of official heritage listing, it is the substantial cost of ongoing maintenance that poses the biggest threat to its survival. The Nylex company, having gone into voluntary administration, could no longer afford the electricity bill (estimated at between $20,000–30,000 per year). This led to the sign being unplugged in March 2009.

Since then, the growing public outcry for the Nylex signage to be relit has gained momentum. Even the company that bought the rights to the Nylex name and clock, Wet Technologies Australia, has been looking for co-sponsors, hoping to repeat the success of the funding partnerships that have kept the Skipping Girl sign alight – 'We'd dearly love to turn it on, but we can't afford the costs. It's incredibly expensive … We are aware how many people want it on … but we're going to need some help'.[4]

These days you don't even have to go to Richmond, or even Melbourne, to see the Nylex sign. Not only does it appear in digital form on Flickr web pages, but it can be seen in a more tangible form on countless homeware products, including tea towels, cushions and teacups. It was even reportedly the source of inspiration for the naming of the acclaimed local architectural practice, Six Degrees. According to principal James Legge, during a naming session at their original Richmond premises one of the architects glanced up at the Nylex clock, and noticed the current temperature was 6 degrees.

OPPOSITE
Original drawings of the Nylex sign featuring the original slab serif lettering *Image: Courtesy of National Trust of Australia (Victoria)*

ABOVE
The Nylex tea towel designed by Make Me Iconic. *Image: Courtesy of Natasha Skunca*

RIGHT
A striking resemblance –the Nuttelex signage *Image: Lan Huang Courtesy of Letterbox*

Situated only a block or so away from the famed Nylex sign stands the distinctive Nuttelex signage, offering the passer-by another illuminated visual spectacle, from its three-dimensional 'squirrel with a schoolbag' and accompanying titling on Church Street to the strikingly solid script letterforms on the side street.

The two signs share an uncannily similar typographic style. Early documentation and sketches of the original Nylex sign dating from 1961 (opposite) show the widely proportioned slab serif typeface is virtually identical to the then-existing Nuttelex signage.

The fact that the names Nuttelex and Nylex share so many letters in common (both begin with an N and end with 'lex') only reinforces speculation of design influence between the two signs.

Design comparisons can no longer be made as the original Nylex sign was reconstructed in a completely different typeface, *Helvetica*, in 1970.

The "Nylex Plastics" sign in Richmond facing the new Morshead Overpass and the South-Eastern Freeway is 120 feet above ground level at its base. The sign itself is 62 feet high to the top of the clock giving an overall height of 182 feet — one of the highest Neon Signs in Australia.

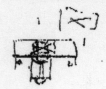

NEON ELECTRIC SIGNS LIMITED
Specialists in Illuminated Signs for over 30 years.
Telephone: 69 3143 (5 lines).
cnr. Cecil and Whiteman Streets, South Melbourne, Victoria.

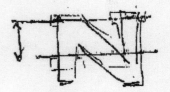

upper echelons

From the top the number stand it was, below 7 Guest seaters

Stand was constructed, built 2 visible fixture on the skyline in line

with the bowlers arm. Sports commentators, after returned to it

such as Lou Richards, and

Little Audrey

The Skipping Girl Vinegar sign has never been very far away from controversy – from the long fight for its restoration right through to working out just who Little Audrey actually is...

No other signage has been so embraced by the Melbourne public as 'Little Audrey', the animated neon sign that looks down upon Victoria Street in the inner-city suburb of Abbotsford. From her origins in the mid-1930s to the present day, Little Audrey's life as a landmark sign has been dramatic and controversial.

Installed in 1936, the original Skipping Girl Vinegar sign first sat on top of the Nycander and Co. Vinegar factory at 627 Victoria Street (on the corner of Walmer Street). Claiming the status of being the first animated neon sign in Australia, Little Audrey depicts a young girl wearing a red dress and red ribbons in her hair, who, through a set of three rapid neon displays is seen jumping over her skipping rope. At the base of the sign sit painted letters highlighted with neon that spell out 'Vinegar'.

Viewed from the perspective of contemporary branding, the Skipping Girl sign is curious. The connection between a skipping girl and vinegar has never been made clear, although the byline that accompanied the initial logo was 'Why is she looking so happy?' 'Because she knows that everybody likes her', suggesting an attempt at linking social popularity with vinegar, this being reinforced by its presence on the product packaging for several decades before the signage was installed.

But just who is the Skipping Girl?

It seems this seemingly simple question is anything but. Over the history of the signage there have been three claims to her identity. Many believe that the original skipping girl was modelled on 8-year-old Kitty Minogue (c.1905–84) after her brother, Jim, sketched her in a winning competition entry for the vinegar company. She later followed a higher calling, becoming Sister Felicitas in the Brigidine Congregation of Nuns.

Others have claimed that the inspiration behind the Skipping Girl sign involved Alma Burns (unknown–1982). Alma lived at the back of a nearby milk bar called the Cosy Corner and would often skip in the street outside. It is said that the vinegar factory manager, mindful of updating the company logo to signage, used Alma as a model for the drawings of the structure.

The third claim came from Irene Barron (1922–), a junior artist at Claude Neon when the sign was being designed in 1936. According to Irene: 'I had to skip 'cause I was the youngest and so I skipped to get the animation of the frock, the rope and my feet'. Perhaps the truth lies somewhere between all three claims – that one girl inspired the initial vinegar logo drawing, while another modelled for the signage itself.

The vinegar itself had an odd effect on the signage. Vinegar fumes from the factory below regularly eroded the copper electrodes in the neon tubing, giving birth to such affectionate descriptions as 'Little Miss Headless' or 'One legged Audrey'. One of the neon maintenance men even recalls,

I remember turning up there one day and there were three dead blokes there. One guy had got into the vinegar vat when they were cleaning out the sludge. He collapsed because of the fumes. Another bloke crawled in to get him and he went as well. And then the son of the bloke who owned Nycander went in there and it killed him too.[1]

In 1968 the tale of the Skipping Girl took another turn. The Nycander Vinegar Company moved their premises to Altona and the Abbotsford site was sold to the Metropolitan Fire Brigade.

The old factory building was demolished, but not before the Skipping Girl sign had been removed and, in the absence of any specific conditions (therefore all salvaged material belonged to the wrecker), Little Audrey was sold by the infamous Whelan the Wrecker to a car wrecker, Mr Doug Snowdon, for just $100. This was perhaps the lowest point in the existence of the Skipping Girl.

It is said that upon discovering the remains of the original 'Little Audrey' signage at Whelan's wreckers yard, Barry Humphries lay a wreath and composed *The Ode to the Skipping Girl*

PREVIOUS PAGES
Joyce Legg, 87, looks at the partly restored Skipping Girl neon sign which was possibly modelled on her late sister Elma Burns (2009) *Image: Craig Abraham, Fairfax Photos*

OPPOSITE
Going ... Going ... Gone; How *The Sun* newspaper reported the demise of the original Skipping Girl Vinegar sign (9 October 1968, p.35) *Image: State Library of Victoria Newspapers Collection, Courtesy of the Herald & Weekly Times Pty Ltd*

GOING . . . GOING . . .

AFTER more than 30 years of skipping up and down on the one spot, the Skipping Girl of Abbotsford has gone from the city skyline. She came down yesterday during the demolition of the vinegar factory whose product she advertised for so long. The company has moved its factory to Altona . . . but there won't be room there for the Skipping Girl. Here's how she made her farewell. LEFT: She stands in place as preparations are made to remove her.

THE Skipping Girl begins her descent as a crane lifts her clear of her perch high above Victoria St., Abbotsford. She was designed by Mr Les Rees, of Neon Electric Signs Ltd. Fittingly, he was there with a camera to record her last moments yesterday.

HER privileged view high over the city has gone. The Skipping Girl stares over a tin fence. When workmen had completed lowering her they found the little girl wasn't quite so little. She stood 25 ft. high.

Pictures: GEORGE BUGDEN
Report: TONY HITCHIN

in her honour.[2]

Part of the ode goes:
The trams are still sage green and pretty
And the roof of the Shrine has been polished
Most of the rest of our city
Has either been ruined or demolished.

For though progress can sometimes be tawdry
Our town planners are brilliant and clever,
Though I privately pray little Audrey
Will outshine them and skip on forever.[3]

The absence of the Skipping Girl created public outcry, even including one radio station, which launched a 'Save Little Audrey the Skipping Girl' campaign. Vinegar manufacturers Mauri Brothers & Thompson had taken over Nycander and negotiations began to create a similar sign. Three sites were unsuccessfully proposed.

Local businessman John Benjamin offered Mauri Brothers a long lease for the sign on top of his Crusader Plate Co. at 651 Victoria Street, approximately 200 metres from the original site. Unfortunately this second location was at a lower height, thereby reducing visibility of the sign. A slightly smaller replica of 'Little Audrey' (now featuring longer hair and a dress that billowed higher at the back) was built and mounted on the new site and launched with a rooftop party in November 1970. And so it was that the switch was flicked

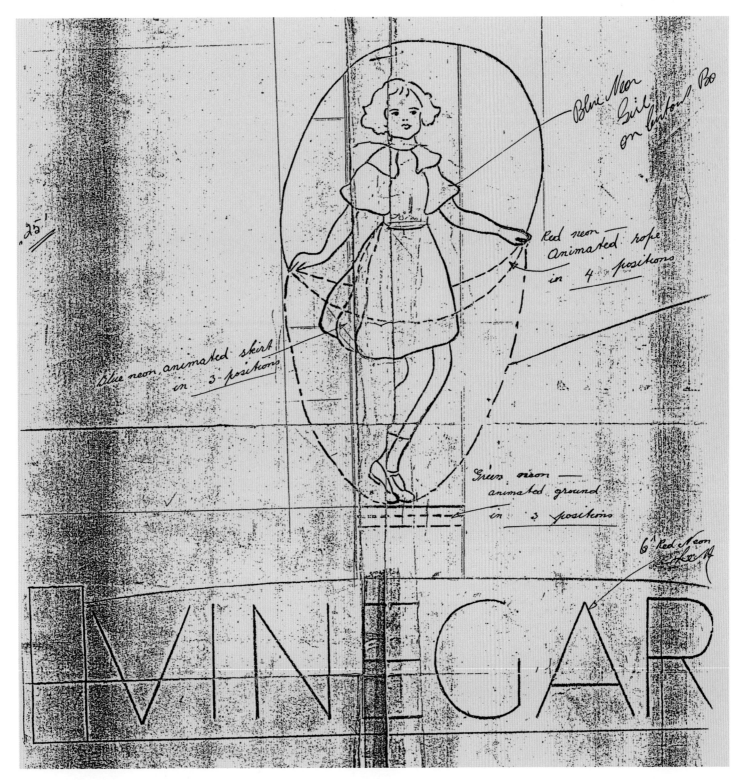

Skipping through time

1936
The original Skipping Girl Vinegar sign, affectionately known as 'Little Audrey', is erected above the Nycander and Co. Pty Ltd factory at 627 Victoria Street on the corner of Walmer Street, Abbotsford. Advertising the company's brand of vinegar, it is believed to be the first animated neon sign in Australia. Built and owned by Neon Electric Signs Pty Ltd, it is leased to Nycander Vinegar for £8, 15p per month.

Early 1960s
Nycander and Co. Pty Ltd is bought out by Mauri Brothers and Thompson.

1968
Nycander and Co. Pty Ltd move their premises to Altona. The Abbotsford site is sold to the Metropolitan Fire Brigade. Whelan the Wrecker demolishes the factory, removes the original Skipping Girl sign and sells it for $100.

1970
Huge public outcry, including a radio campaign to save the sign. A smaller replica sign (with modifications) is built and mounted on the rooftop of 651 Victoria Street. A 25-year lease for the new sign is signed. 'Little Audrey' is relit.

1971
The new sign wins first prize in the roof section of the National Outdoor Advertising Sign competition.

1974
In May comedian Barry Humphries purportedly finds the remains of the original Skipping Girl sign, lays a wreath and composes the song 'Ode to the Skipping Girl' in her honour.

back on and the new 'Little Audrey' remained alight and skipping for another 16 years.

In 1986 the Crusader Plate Company closed down and the Skipping Girl sign was once again turned off and in limbo. Within a year the building had been sold to the construction company Hooker Cockram, who eventually converted it into offices, appropriately naming the new development 'Skipping Girl Place'.

Despite this recognition, as well as the sign being officially listed by the National Trust (Victoria) in 2000, by 2001 the lease on the sign had expired and with nobody to take it over it once again faded from the night sky.

By 2005 a support group known as the 'Friends of Audrey', had mounted a public petition, which was signed by over 3000 people to lobby the National Trust for further protection and restoration. This led to its inclusion on Victoria's Heritage Register in 2007 and the launching of a campaign by the National Trust (Victoria) and the Heritage Council of Victoria the following year calling for Melbournians to 'Help Audrey skip again'.

By 2009 sufficient funds had been raised and there was enough corporate support for the restoration of this iconic structure. It involved an array of interested parties, including energy company AGL, National Trust (Victoria), Heritage Council of Victoria, the Melbourne Restoration Fund, 'Friends of Audrey', the public and the Skipping Girl owners' representatives, Spring & Parks Pty Ltd. On 23 March the sign was removed to be fully restored by Delta Neon. On 10 June then Energy and Resources Minister Peter Bachelor flicked the switch on to once again relight 'Little Audrey'.

As a nod to further modernisation, the Skipping Girl is now powered by renewable energy.

To this very day mystery surrounds the whereabouts of the original Skipping Girl sign. One story claims that she sat rusting away in a farmer's shed in Central Victoria before being taken to her final resting place at the bottom of Stawell tip. Whether true or not, this speculation, like the real identity of Audrey, keeps the Skipping Girl Vinegar sign one of the most vivid and intriguing stories of Melbourne.

A NEON MAINTENANCE MAN RECALLS:
'There used to be a door in the bottom of her skirt with two 1500 volt leads. I'd be standing up there with my arm through the bottom door fixing it all up and all the louts going past in their cars would be yelling 'Ya' filthy f**in' bastard'.[4]

PAGE 156
Audrey goes off to Whelan the Wrecker, October 1968, from the *Port of Melbourne Quarterly*, Oct–Dec 1980 (vol 29, N° 10) *Image: Courtesy of Port of Melbourne Corporation, State Library of Victoria La Trobe Collection*

PAGE 157
Original sketches of the Skipping Girl Vinegar neon sign *Image: Courtesy National Trust of Australia (Victoria)*

OPPOSITE
The restored Skipping Girl Vinegar neon sign being lowered into place during its 2009 re-installation *Image: Jesse Marlow*

1986
Crusader Plate Co. factory closes and the Skipping Girl sign is switched off.

1987
'Little Audrey' appears in the TV film 'Bachelor Girl'.

1988
Crusader Plate Co. building is sold to construction company Hooker Cockram Ltd.

1990
The site is redeveloped into offices and named 'Skipping Girl Place'. The restored sign is ceremoniously re-lit.

2000
The 1970 replica Skipping Girl sign is listed by the National Trust (Victoria).

2001
The contract for the sign expires and the sign is once again switched off.

2002
Skipping Girl is referenced in the lyrics of the song 'It's all in the way' by My Friend the Chocolate Cake.

2003
Abbotsford resident Jenny Hume and two friends, Tricia Broadbent and Pat Cowl, form the group 'Friends of Audrey' to raise awareness and support to protect and restore the sign.

2004
Named after the iconic sign, Melbourne band 'Skipping Girl Vinegar' is formed.

2005
'Friends of Audrey' collect 3000 signatures for a petition to the National Trust calling for the sign's protection and repair.

2007
The sign is added to the National Trust's official list of state heritage icons and included on Victoria's Heritage Register.

2008
On 6 May the National Trust (Victoria) and the Heritage Council of Victoria launch the Skipping Girl Appeal, calling for Melbournians to 'Help Audrey skip again'.

2009
Enough funds are raised for the restoration of 'Little Audrey'. The sign is removed on 23 March and fully restored by Delta Neon. On 10 June 'Little Audrey' is relit, powered by renewable energy.

The 'other' girl

Comparisons between the Skipping Girl and the St Moritz Skating Girl highlight very different fates. While the former has been lovingly and expensively restored, re-installed and celebrated by an adoring public, the latter was removed from its site and is currently stored in the St Kilda Historical Society 'dungeons'.[1]

OPPOSITE
The St. Moritz skating rink façade, featuring the glowing neon skating girls flanking the rooftop building titling
Image: Courtesy of St. Kilda Historical Collection

Once a vibrant destination for visitors to seaside St Kilda, the Art Deco-period St Moritz Skating Rink operated from 1939 to 1981. The rink could hold up to 2000 people and held 1850 square metres of ice.[2] The building was demolished in 1982 to make way for a hotel development, first the St Moritz Hotel, and then later the Novotel Hotel.

An electrician by the name of Tom Ingram rushed to save what he could. He climbed a ladder 6 metres up the façade and unbolted two neon skating signs. Each of these signs stood 1.7 metres tall. The signs he called 'the girls', were in poor condition, their surfaces pitted and the neon broken.

They were stored away in Ingram's shed until 1991, when he was asked by the owners of the St Moritz Hotel to remake the signage. The rust was cleaned off, holes filled, new neon installed and surfaces repainted. The signage was then installed in a new glass display cabinet and the Skating Girl was reborn.

The renewed signage hung in the hotel café until the business changed hands. Not fitting in with the new owner's decor, it was covered up by panels for eight years and almost forgotten about until a chance conversation between Tom and one of the bar staff.[3] It was uncovered and donated to the St Kilda Historical Society in 2005. And there it still sits in storage.[4]

While most people know of Skipping Girl and some know of the St Moritz Skating Girl, not many people realise that there was once a third animated neon girl lighting up the Melbourne night sky – the State Savings Bank Girl.

Neon girl trio

Erected on 8 October 1957 beside the Abbotsford Bridge, she faced the downhill traffic heading into the city from the eastern suburbs. In this position she was visible from the crest of Studley Park Road and beyond. The neon girl, 5.4 metres wide and 2.7 metres tall, went through an animated sequence of dropping pennies (each 60 cm in diameter) into a money box measuring some 1.8 metres by 1.5 metres. Below this sat the title 'State Savings Bank', delivering a memorable, if not slightly literal, message to encourage people to 'save your pennies'.

The Bank Girl was the brainchild of Mr A. E. Hocking, chairman of the Commissioners of the State Savings Bank, who had always been impressed with the Skipping Girl Vinegar sign. However, not long after her installation it was thought that her face looked too witch-like, so it was eventually replaced with a gentler version in May 1959.

Even with her new soft face she continued to receive a mixed reaction from the public. In March 1961 a paragraph in the *Herald* complained that the pennies were not dropping properly.

On another occasion someone wrote to the bank commenting that the coins featured 'heads' on both sides.

On 18 June 1964, only seven years after her first public appearance, the State Savings Bank contacted the makers of the sign, Claude Neon, and requested its removal. It had apparently been giving trouble for some time and the ongoing maintenance costs were not seen as worth the effort. The State Savings Bank Girl was never seen again.

OPPOSITE
All that remains of the State Savings Bank Girl neon signage, the original Claude Neon drawings (c. 1957)
Image: State Library of Victoria Pictures Collection Courtesy of Claude Neon
H95.83/9

In 1989 plans were made to install a neon sign of a naked woman on top of one of Australia's most famous hotels, the Young and Jackson Hotel on the north-west corner of Flinders and Swanston Streets, Melbourne's busiest intersection.[1]

However, this was going to be no ordinary neon sign. It was to be based on the hotel's famous long-term resident, *Chloe* (1875), a French painting by Jules Joseph Lefebvre depicting a nymph-like nude young woman that has been on show in the hotel since 1909. Although the 'Neon Chloe' was never approved by the authorities, the debate generated a great deal of publicity for the hotel and served to maintain a deep public moral division on the issue of exhibition of nudity. Given its prime position, the Young and Jackson Hotel has long been associated with advertising, particularly neon and electric skysigns, above its façade. This has made the landmark the focus of many battles between those who support and those who despise signage.

Greens Councillor, Fraser Brindley, considers the Young and Jackson Hotel as the city's worst example of 'advertising gone mad'.

You stand there with St Paul's Cathedral, Federation Square, Flinders Street Station, then whack, a huge billboard ... It's the epitome of appalling outdoor advertising.[2]

In 2008 Cody Outdoor Advertising submitted a planning proposal for the installation of the latest billboard incarnation, a roof-mounted major promotion electronic message display (EMD) to wrap around the corner of the building end to end. Their method of persuasion was lateral, cleverly claiming that 'commercial signs have also played an important role in establishing Young and Jackson's landmark quality'.[3]

This introduced a whole new perspective on the debate, that rather than signage detracting from the streetscape, they are part of the streetscape. Taking this argument to its logical end, the social heritage of advertising was used to justify its ongoing presence.

The application was successful and the spectacular message display was installed soon after. The design of the huge electronic display is itself very innovative (see page 25).

Rather than a conventional square finish, the digital billboard area tapers off each of its ends through a series of square gaps of increasing frequency, inferring pixels. The advertisement images therefore have to be specifically designed to accommodate these areas and run on a schedule of 8 seconds per message before moving onto the next one.

Because the technology allows for this infinitely dynamic display of different advertising messages, the Young and Jackson's sign is considered to be one of Australia's infinitely lucrative billboards, charging out its 37-metre expanse for $10,000 a week, and bringing in an estimated $4 million dollars a year.[4]

Naked, Young and Jackson

Just how close did Melbourne come to having a 3.5 metre tall naked woman in neon overlooking its busiest intersection?

OPPOSITE
The Young and Jackson Hotel, Melbourne (c. 1969) *Image: Angus O'Callaghan from 'Marvellous Melbourne' Collection. Courtesy Kozminsky Gallery*

FOLLOWING PAGE
Princes Bridge (c. 1969) *Image: Angus O'Callaghan from 'Marvellous Melbourne' Collection. Courtesy Kozminsky Gallery*

She's cravin' me

Craven A Filter was one of the largest roadside signs ever made. It was just over Princes Bridge at the start of the railway. Had over 800 bloody globes in it. Late one night I was working on it and I was that bloody tired. Rang my missus and said, 'I won't be home tonight. I'm going to sleep with this sheila called Craven A. She's cravin' for me.' She asked where I was and I said, 'I'm sitting up in the sign above the Yarra River and I've got about an hour of work to do. I'll have a sleep here tonight.' So I crawled into the corner, put my toolbag under my head and didn't wake up until eight the next morning.

Ian 'Podgy' Rogers | NEON MAINTENANCE MAN

Art or billboard?

Just when you thought that product placement was a relatively new advertising phenomena, evidence of it happening some 80 years ago can still be seen on the Neo-Classical façade of Newspaper House.

Built in an age when the title or purpose of a building was proudly etched into its façade, the function of Newspaper House is self-explanatory. The architects of the building's refurbished façade, Stephenson & Meldrum, won the commission in 1933 through a public competition run by the building's owners, *The Herald*.

The most immediate feature of Newspaper House is the extraordinary tiled mosaic that runs the entire width of its street frontage. Created by the leading Neo-Classical mural artist Napier Waller (1893–1972), *I'll put a girdle round about the Earth* is a jubilant celebration of people's potential to use technology for both material and spiritual fulfillment.

Waller's work is calmly classical, using timeless and heroic figure compositions to express ideas and ideals; deep-seated mythologies shared by pagan and Christian experience; dreams of a wondrous past and a perfected future.[1]

He worked using only his left arm, the other having been amputated after injury during active service in the First World War.

But it is in Waller's clever accommodation of two front windows where the mosaic wraps around the sills and edges that some lesser known design details can be seen – namely the exact date of the mosaic installation, cryptically concealed in a line of sturdy block sans serif titling.

Waller was selected for the project by one of Melbourne's more enlightened arts patrons of the time, Theodore Fink, who also happened to be a director of *The Herald* newspaper. For the observant viewer, the dues to the patron are paid for all to see.

Placed in a prime position just behind the composition's central figure, amid modern airships, railways, telephone poles and the busy cogs of industry, is a newspaper whose prominent and legible masthead, *The Herald*, can be seen to

personify the socially and industrially progressive essence of the design.

Despite its classical beauty and technical complexity, Waller's mosaic for Newspaper House could possibly be noted as one of the earliest forms of 'product placement' in art and architecture.

Although Waller's mosaic is the most immediate and eye-catching feature of Newspaper House, the building's typographic titling is also of significance.

Positioned at the very top of the façade, high above eye-height and almost entirely obscured by trees, it is a unique example of electric neon being architecturally integrated into a building façade, just as it appears in the architect's drawings of the proposed building in 1932. It is also said to be the oldest surviving neon in Melbourne.

What's the time?
It's a B past an M.

The industry of Richmond runs like clockwork.
But these clocks don't have numerals, they have letters.

'Look for the Red Globe, the signal sign of supremacy' announced the invitation from the Dimmeys Drapery Emporium catalogue of the 1920s. Although the fortunes of the Dimmeys empire have wavered throughout its history, the building, the tower and its globe have indeed remained a familiar landmark of Richmond to this day. Described by one architect as an eclectic mix of Romanesque, Classical and Byzantine themes,[1] the tower on which the globe sits also features a clock, a civic feature common at the time it was built. The size of the clock face was remarked upon, proudly claiming that it was '9 inches larger than the clock at the Melbourne Town Hall'.[2]

However, it was in the 1960s that the clock took on a distinctly typographic persona. The roman numerals for each hour were replaced by 12 letters to read: DIMMEYSTORES. Although this new feature capitalised on its landmark status, the new talking point had been inspired by another 'typo-clock' built some 40 years earlier only a few blocks away and well within sight of Dimmeys.

The Richmond factory of match manufacturer Bryant & May had installed a clock tower in 1922 featuring the 12 letters BRYANT&MAYPL, representing the numerals on its illuminated clock face.

Around the same time as Dimmeys was 'paying homage' to Bryant & May, a more public typo-clock was being installed (or grown) at the Royal Botanic Gardens. Presented to Melbourne by Swiss watchmakers in 1966, the Melbourne Floral Clock also features finely manicured letters as the radial measure of time. To this very day it is replanted annually into new typographic configurations.

A taste for typographic clocks had actually emerged in Melbourne some decades earlier. A poster advertising the then newly developing housing estate of Hawthorn in 1925 depicts a figure moving the hands of a large clock, whose numerals have been replaced with the word 'opportunity' (curiously enough an 11-letter word).

Time is money

By the mid-twentieth century there was a firm financial partnership between signage and public time-keeping. The income derived from advertising could be used to subsidise the construction and ongoing maintenance of these clocks. Over time, this relationship developed well beyond an economic one as the clocks gradually became public landmarks, acquiring commonly known nicknames such as the 'Nylex clock', 'Ampol clock' and 'Coca-Cola clock'.

In the public eye, this graphic combination of letters (signage) and numbers (clock) became a ubiquitous feature in the everyday visual landscape. Signage/clock combinations featuring figurative elements brought this association even closer to the public's heart with many signs anthropomorphised into much-loved urban 'characters'. The combination of all of these reinforced public notions of signage's civic purpose and benefits beyond their initial intention of advertising.

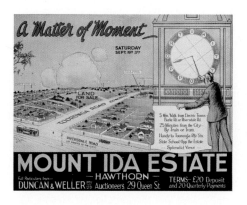

OPPOSITE
One of the most
prominent city 'signage
clocks' was the Ampol
Clock in Swanston Street.
(1966) K.J. Halla, negative
*Image: State Library of
Victoria Pictures Collection*
H36133/80

THIS PAGE
South Melbourne's
'Coca-Cola clock' always
suggested that it was time
for a drink (c. 1962)
Lyle Fowler, negative
(touched up) *Image: State
Library of Victoria Pictures
Collection* H92.20/7285

Buildings and letters have always had a lot in common.
Both concern themselves with a human dimension,
scale and proportion; both are structural and purpose-
built; and both carry with them long-established
histories and conventions that perpetually tempt
reinterpretation, even subversion. So it's not at
all surprising that the worlds of architecture and
typography should come together in a single term –

Typotecture

Although a common feature in our streetscape, the nature of typotecture ranges from the intensely typographic (letters forming the very basis of a building), the boldly typographic (buildings making bold, even monumental statements), right through to the suggestively typographic (those buildings that feature gently integrated letterforms).

A close relationship with letters is certainly not a new phenomenon in the field of architecture. Many of the monumental arches of the Roman period were essentially bold typographic proclamations of military victories supported by cleverly engineered architectural forms. Such monumental typographic gestures have continued throughout human history, most notably by the Italian fascist leader Mussolini, who ordered the construction of massive archways in the shape of the letter 'M' under which his theatrical procession would drive, proclaiming absolute power. The use of his strikingly symmetrical initial 'M' was serendipitous, perfectly suiting the expression of a brutally geometric neo-classical sense of (social) order.

Grand typographic statements built into a solid structure continue in architectural practice today. Only now such bold typotecture expresses corporate interests as well as public ones, reflecting a shift in authority from civic bodies to the private sector.

One of the most intriguing local examples of typotecture is the 'FLIP' signage, designed by Ashton Raggatt McDougall (ARM), that sits on top of the north-western corner of the Melbourne Central shopping complex on the corner of Elizabeth and La Trobe Streets.

Adorning its dense skeletal structure, these huge bright red geometric letterforms spell out the words FLIP twice, with two of the letterforms, the 'F' and 'P' being themselves flipped upside-down. Naturally enough, the viewer assumes these forms as signage, but after noticing that there are no correspondingly named stores on the corner, one is then left to wonder as its purpose.

When asked about the meaning of these giant letterforms, ARM Design director, Neil Masterton, responded with a quotation from Lewis Carroll's *Through the Looking Glass and What Alice Found There* – "That's the effect of living backwards, the Queen said kindly. It always makes one a little giddy at first."[1] Comparing the apparent symmetry of the FLIP signage to a Rorschach inkblot personality test, he described it as 'not completely right but surely not totally wrong'.[2]

Richmond's V and X Building (as it is affectionately known) is similarly obtuse in its use of large-scale typography. A massive V and an X graphically distinguish the façades of the two buildings, while huge letter Y shapes jut out from the back of the complex. Developed in the early 2000s, these typographic giants seek to readily identify and re-market what was once the Melbourne headquarters of Siemens. Project architect, Paul Hede from Hede Architects, reflected:

Everybody knew the building as the Siemens building because of its huge sign. We decided to use that same typographic language to revolutionalise the building. We decided to use the letter X for the larger of the buildings and V for the smaller because a V is basically half an X.[3]

This motif is extended throughout the entire complex, right through to the door handles, which are shaped as a X or a V.

It's a combination of architecture and branding. Because the building was now multi-tenancy it was important to create an architectural identity that exists beyond just one company. So now tenants can describe their address as 'X3' – meaning the third floor of the X building, and so on.[4]

When asked as to why the letters X, V and Y were specifically chosen, his instant response was typically architectural: 'because of the beautiful broad symmetry'.

Another example of a bold typographic industrial statement taking architectural form was the ETA Foods Factory (1957), designed by Grounds, Romberg and Boyd. Its tubular bracing formed arrows directing the viewer's eye to the big red E, T and A spelt out in large moulded plastic letters. The striking architectural strategy transformed the factory façade into a massive curtain billboard, giving it a distinctive presence to the nearby highway traffic. Thought to be one of the first examples of 'supergraphics', the lineal nature of the three letterforms

PREVIOUS PAGE
Southland Shopping
Centre, Cheltenham
(1969) Wolfgang Sievers
Photograph, gelatin silver
*Image: State Library of
Victoria Pictures Collection*
H98.30/312

OPPOSITE TOP AND
BOTTOM LEFT
A section of the dramatic
'FLIP' typography at
Melbourne Central
(2008) Architects: Ashton
Raggatt McDougall
*Image: Tim Fluence
Courtesy of Letterbox*

OPPOSITE BOTTOM RIGHT
The V and X building,
Richmond (2011)
Architects: Hede Architects
*Image: Lan Huang
Courtesy of Letterbox*

FACTORY FOR MARRICKVILLE MARGARINE PTY.LTD. & NUT FOODS PTY.LTD. AT BRAYBROOK, VIC.

NEW PROPOSAL FOR MAIN ENTRANCE.

GROUNDS, ROMBERG & BOYD , ARCHITECTS   340 ALBERT STREET E. MELBOURNE. TELEPHONE JA 5351 JA 5352. OCTOBER 57

OPPOSITE
The ETA factory,
Braybrook (1960)
Wolfgang Sievers
photograph, gelatin silver
*Image: State Library of
Victoria Pictures Collection*
H2000.195/301

THIS PAGE AND OVERLEAF
Details of original sketches of the ETA factory by
the architectural firm Grounds, Romberg and Boyd
(1957–60) *Image: State Library of Victoria Manuscripts
Collection* MS 13363

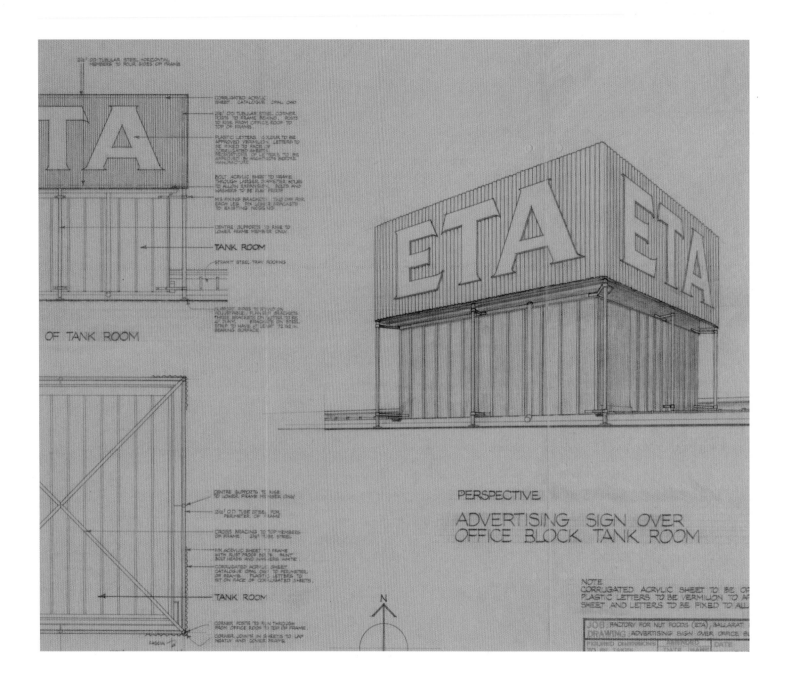

PERSPECTIVE

ADVERTISING SIGN OVER
OFFICE BLOCK TANK ROOM

(none of which feature any curves) reiterates a strong geometry. Appearing in their architectural plans sketched in bright red pencil, this was clearly seen as a key highlight of this innovative building. Although the letters have been removed, the building remains.

More common are the quieter and gentler integrations of letterform and built form, relics of a period when modernity was expressed through the use of simple sans serif titling.

Clear unseriffed letterforms are most legible at a good scale and conform most harmoniously to the geometrical character of contemporary design. Letters set forward from a wall surface or in silhouette above a roof decorate a building without breaking up wall surfaces.[5]

This form of façade titling was at times descriptive, and can be seen in Diamond House (c.1936, built for Dunklings Jewellers) and Lyric House (c.1929, built along a musical theme for Wertheim Pianos), while others followed popular national motifs, such as the smooth 'rising sun' roofline typography of the Sun Theatre (c.1938).[6] Such statements of permanence lent the buildings an immediate identity and purpose, both in content and form. The confident block sans titling across the rear of the Big Store in Prahran shows that it is not just the front of buildings that deserve such definition.

Although less conventional, the rough-hewn titling on the old Myer Dispatch Centre (c.1929) in Carlton presents a

TOP AND BOTTOM LEFT
The structural permancy of the Diamond House titling, along with lesser-seen traces of other signage on its side, still gives a strong indication as to the original purpose of the building (2011) *Images: Lan Huang Courtesy of Letterbox*

BOTTOM RIGHT
Diamond House (c.1957)
Lyle Fowler
Negative, flexible base
Image: State Library of Victoria Pictures Collection
H92.20/6028

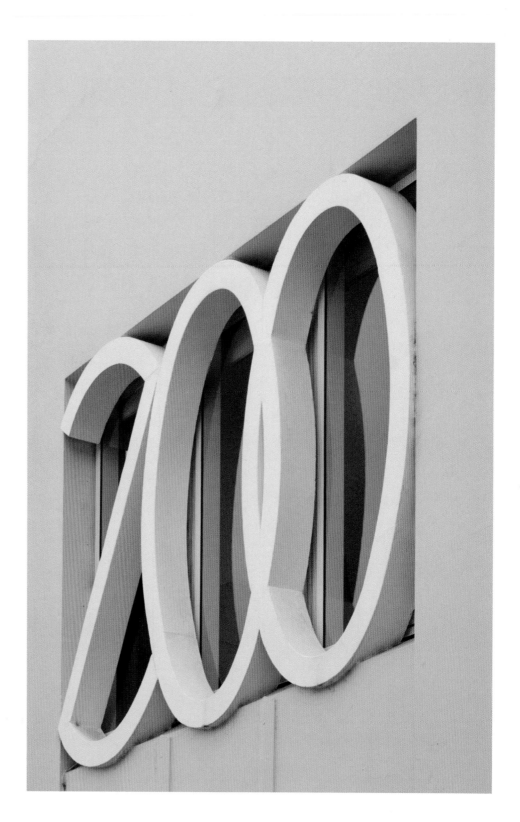

rather incongruous typographic representation of the Melbourne department store empire. Its incongruous appeal speaks of a period prior to modern 'total' identity design where visual consistency is considered paramount. Even the recent renovation of the Myer façade in Bourke Street features a structural typographic reference. What at first appear to be a series of black zigzags across the long glass awning is in fact a series of Ms, perfectly reflecting the proportions of the very early 'M' monogram featured near the main entrance to the department store.

Another of ARM's trademark typographic contributions to architectural form is to be found at the refurbished Melbourne Shrine of Remembrance. The entranceway to the undercroft information centre features the sombre Anzac phrase 'Lest we forget' written in large letters across its angled walls. Presented in a handwritten style, it is as though an entry from a soldier's private diary has been magnified to an architectural scale. This work succeeds on a dual level: its scale is both public and striking, yet privately quiet and poignant. ARM Director Ian McDougall explains the appeal of combining typography and architecture:

> *The opportunity to treat a built object as an enormous page is just too tempting. We know the urge to 'say something' by inscribing it onto a surface predates architecture, so our desire to communicate in this way seems to have primal origins.*[7]

Perhaps the most whimsical typotecture is to be found at Melbourne Zoo. Built in the 1930s by the Victorian Public Works Department, its striking entrance is marked by three large uppercase letters that spell out ZOO, their forms perfectly curved to reflect the surrounding Art Deco roundness. The result is suitably playful and harmonious. Playful lettering also appeared on the old Zoo railway station kiosk. Built to service train-travelling zoo visitors, it welcomed them with the word KIOSK painted as a series of animal bones.

So what does typotecture tell us? Above all, it indicates an architectural commitment to permanence, both civic or commercial. Such investment is now rare. We live in the era of privatising civic infrastructure, corporate headquarters readily moved for economic advantage elsewhere, while the constant renaming of sports stadiums and other large infrastructure reflects the transient nature of sponsorship deals.

And with the passing of this age of permanence, signage and architecture forms become more temporary, portable or even modular in nature. What the readymade tilt-slab wall is to architecture, vinyl lettering is to signage. Both indicate an economic reluctance to invest in a longer-term sense of place. And with this goes a sense of collective memory.

OPPOSITE LEFT
The Royal Park railway zoo kiosk featuring a playful 'bone' type style. This photograph was taken in 1993. It was demolished soon after. *Image: Author*

OPPOSITE
The main entrance signage at the Melbourne Zoo makes great use of typographic geometry (2010) *Image: Lan Huang Courtesy of Letterbox*

TOP
The old Myer Dispatch Centre offers a unique typographic tone (2011)

MIDDLE
Renovations to the Myer façade reflect the older signage monogram form (2011) *Images: Lan Huang Courtesy of Letterbox*

BOTTOM
The dramatic script used for 'Lest we forget' at the Melbourne Shrine of Remembrance Information Centre by Ashton Raggett McDougall (2010) *Image: Author*

OPPOSITE
Sun Theatre
Yarraville (c.1995)
Warren Kirk
*Image: State Library of
Victoria Pictures Collection*
H95.225/8

THIS PAGE
Majestic Theatre
Flinders St Melbourne
(c.1936) Commercial
Photographic Co.
photograph, gelatin silver
*Image: State Library of
Victoria Pictures Collection*
H2009.185/15

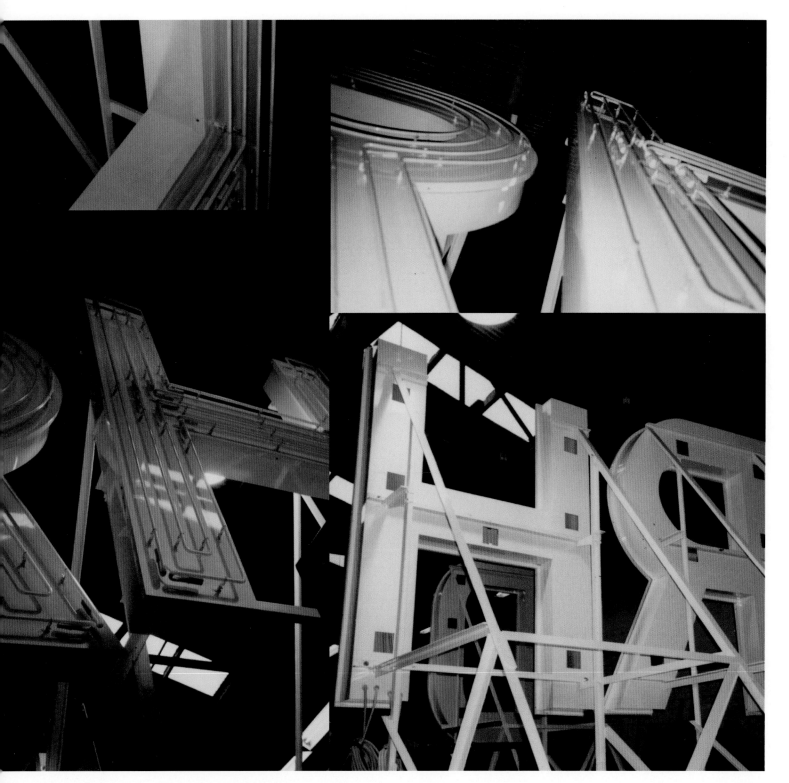

The big steal

Typographic crime is rare. But when the stolen items stand metres high and weigh a few tonnes it's an extraordinary feat.

While cycling through Collingwood one afternoon, graphic designer Andrew Budge glimpsed something intriguing through the doors of an old factory workshop – a set of massive sans serif capital letterforms, all fixed to a skysign metal frame. Further enquiry revealed that this was the newly reconstructed signage from the iconic *Herald Sun* Building.

Featuring four strips of neon, each letter stood 2 metres tall. Since the 1923 Flinders Street headquarters of the *Herald Sun* newspaper were vacated by its original occupants and converted into boutique apartments, the original signage, considered to be an intrinsic feature, was also up for renewal. The letters were showing signs of their considerable vintage, and, because of their position over one of Melbourne's major thoroughfares, were even thought by some to constitute a public safety risk.

The *Herald Sun* signage, said to be the longest neon skysign in Melbourne still in existence, sits above the building looking south over the Jolimont rail yards and the Yarra River. Widely acknowledged as an integral feature of the Melbourne skyline, these nine luminous letters from the *Herald Sun* Building were now well beyond salvaging – each letter would have to completely reconstructed, meticulously matched to its original.

According to NTA Signs, the firm undertaking this reconstruction project, this specialist work was just the beginning of the story. While the signage was being painstakingly reproduced, six of the nine original letters went missing from their factory car park in Collingwood. Nothing odd about that, except that the culprits would have needed a crane and several semitrailers to remove them.

Clearly it was not the work of an opportunist, but a rare case of typographic theft. The police were notified and were on the lookout for individuals who may have recently acquired some rather conspicuous monumental letterforms. Speculation has it that the police were even monitoring the online auction site eBay for leads on the disposal of the stolen goods. To our knowledge the letters have never been found.[1]

On Thursday 14 June 2005 the newborn letters were hoisted on top of the *Herald Sun* Building, glistening in the wet winter afternoon sunlight. This grand installation attracted quite a crowd of onlookers, who were there just to enjoy the spectacle, not knowing that behind this visual splendour lay one of the most mysterious typographic renovations ever carried out.

PAGES 192–193
The reproduction of the Herald Sun letterforms in the NTA workshop (2007) *Images: Andrew Budge, Designland*

OPPOSITE
The newly installed pristine letter 'D' of the Herald Sun signage (2008) *Image: Tim Fluence Courtesy of Letterbox*

THIS PAGE LEFT
The Herald Sun signage (2008) *Image: Tim Fluence Courtesy of Letterbox*

A is for apartment. B is for butchering.

Real estate development can be unkind to signage. The urgency to convert a site from industrial to residential often promotes a 'scorched earth' approach – complete erasure of what once occupied the site. However, amid the crashing bricks and billowing dust there often lie the remnants of perhaps the most identifiable symbol of a building's origins – its signage.

Heritage swallowed by development: council

Picture: ANDREW DE LA RUE

The Victorian Government was compromising one of Melbourne's most important heritage sites by allowing the destruction of an art deco advertising sign, the Historic Buildings Council said yesterday.

The council's chairwoman, Dr Jan Penney, said it had refused permission for developers to destroy the Swallow and Ariell sign of the former Swallow and Ariell Biscuit factory in Port Melbourne because it was a significant Melbourne icon.

Dr Penney said the decision by the Planning Minister, Mr Rob MacLellan, to override the council and allow those transforming the former biscuit factory into residential units to destroy the pressed cement sign would reduce the heritage value of the site.

She said the sign was a "gem of art deco advertising and significant for its simplicity".

"It's a Melbourne icon that has now gone in the same way as the Allen's Sweet sign and other important icons that have been allowed to disappear," Dr Penney said.

She said the council found it impossible to accept that the developers could not incorporate the sign into their plans and rejected their plans to recreate a similar sign on a new wall.

The Swallow and Ariell factory was built in 1854 and in 1883 it was regarded as the fifth largest factory in the world.   —AAP

...e Dvornak, a construction worker, removes letters from the Swallow and Ariell sign at the Port Melbourne factory yesterday.

In the case of readily recognisable sites, the removal of signage can not only strip away a building's identity but also its social role as a landmark. Beyond any conspicuous architectural features specific to its purpose (e.g. a church or power station), very often it is the signage that gives the viewer a sense of the function, history and meaning of a building.

Threaded as it is through the stories of architecture and industrial design, signage can often offer a clear point of reference in ascertaining not just the vintage of a building but its larger social context. Generally, property developers have been slow to realise the economic advantage of retaining signage.

After all, what's in it for them? The short answer to that is, a lot. From the perspective of a potential buyer, what could offer more graphic architectural character than original signage? And from the viewpoint of the developer, this 'purchasable history' brings with it the very things that many buyers are eager to buy into – a sense of authenticity and historical character. At a time when typography is becoming increasingly mainstream in its appeal, it is somewhat ironic that apartment dwellers can furnish their abodes with a sofa range called Helvetica or dry their dishes with a tea towel featuring typeface samplers, while living in a recently converted building stripped of its typographic identity.

Thankfully, things are changing. In the cases of buildings whose titling is completely structurally integrated, the removal of such letterforms is increasingly being seen as a deliberate

and unacceptable act of erasure. This has shifted public perception of what is worth preserving and what is not. Lettering integrated into façades, common during the modernist period, is now widely considered to be a natural extension of architectural preservation.

The conversion of the Swallow & Ariell biscuit factory in Port Melbourne into apartments in the mid-1990s demonstrates the complexity of this relationship. Although the Historical Buildings Council initially argued that the destroying the striking Art Deco

lettering would 'reduce the heritage value' of this very significant 1854 industrial complex, a permit was eventually issued to remove them in 1994. So down came the original pressed cement signage (lettering and swallow bird) over the loading bay. It was only many years later that a faithful replica of this lost signage was then installed over the very same site, now the car park entrance.

But not all the original signage has been re-installed. Adopted as the company's visual identity, the Swallow & Ariell biscuit factory had made a swallow

bird into a prominent local landmark. To proudly mark the seaside factory, a huge swallow-shaped sign was manu-factured and mounted upon a towering pole overlooking the front of the building. Reputed to be visible from ships docking at nearby Station Pier, it was said to spin around, always pointing in the direction of the wind.

Proudly illustrated on the front cover of the company's centenary publication in 1954, the renowned swallow sign vanished in the 1960s, never to be seen again.

When the North Melbourne headquarters of dairy company Bulla Cream was converted into apartments, the developers had the good sense to retain the prominent signage as a feature of the 1928 site. Marketed as the Bulla Cream Apartments, the retention of the prominent signage respectfully continues its function as a local landmark. Other recent industrial-to-residential developments have been more conscious of preserving typographic character. These include Flinders Lane's Duckboard House (where the original idiosyncratic script

signage has been faithfully reproduced), Brunswick's Stawell Buildings, (which features an accurate restoration of the old Whelan the Wrecker's yard signage) and *The Herald Sun* illuminated signage on Flinders Street among many.

But not all developers have grasped the possibilities of retaining typographic character. Dominion House in Flinders Lane, whose balconies mercilessly cut right through the façade titling, stands as a graphic reminder to such insensitivities.

OPPOSITE
Sunshine
(2007)
Louis Porter
Image: Courtesy of artist

LEFT
Aircraft
(2007)
Louis Porter
Image: Courtesy of artist

Take a peek behind many of the building façades you think you know to discover the multi-layered traces of previous lives – this is the typographic archaeology of the *uncovered*.

Peeling the onion

YOFFA HOUSE

Thousands of people walk past it every day and never look up. But it is not the Adelphi Hotel's clean lines of modernity and glistening metallic skin that beckons their eyes upwards. Those who stop and look up at its Flinders Lane façade wonder in awe at the hotel's rooftop swimming pool that overhangs the edge of the building, allowing uniquely voyeuristic perspectives for both swimmer and pedestrian alike. The addition of this public spectacle was added during its conversion from a warehouse into boutique apartments in 1993 by architectural firm Denton Corker Marshall (DCM), whose trademark diagonal forms adorn the front entrance of the hotel.[1] An unintended outcome of the angled signage is that it allows the keen observer to also see an earlier, well-hidden titling featuring the original building name, Yoffa House. The name refers to Ephraim Yoffa (1864–1938), once the owner of Yoffa Hosiery and Knitting Mills, revealing that the building was part of 'Schmatte Business' – the Jewish rag-trade origins of a pre-gentrified Flinders Lane.

This rich history sits just below the surface of the street, its cultural story revealed by its typography. Not only is the name of Yoffa House indicative of a previous street culture and ethnicity, its stylistic appearance also suggests aspects of the time and place. The original signage for the building is cast in a sturdy sans reminescent of Gill Sans, a typeface borne from an emerging English modernism of the late 1920s. Its presence on the metallic façade of a warehouse infers a firm embrace of a modern and efficient productivity.

The uncovered

Known as the 'uncoverings', these are the once-entombed layers of typography momentarily exposed by the demolition of a façade, hoarding or entire building. And because their fragile life-span is defined purely by how long it takes to once again cover them up, their re-exposure can range from many years to a single day. Some are exposed so transiently that in the time it takes to return to the site with a camera they are no longer there. Such uncoverings have become more prevalent in inner-city areas stimulated by 'urban renewal', property speculation and real estate booms.

With their faded complexions once again illuminated by sunlight, the once bold proclamations of these uncoverings now ring out to a changed world. To the contemporary eye many of these are seen

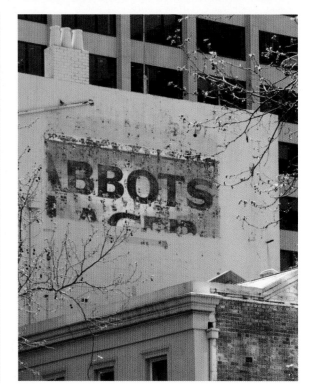

as appealingly quaint and sometimes just plain curious. Collectively, they represent a 'typographic archaeology', an unpeeling of the city, its people and their stories.

Reintroduced into a contemporary environment, these uncoverings offer a rich reading of an area and the lives of the inhabitants, perhaps indicating the lower social status of areas now gentrified, the aspirations of emerging lifestyles and technologies, or directions to a place long gone from the public consciousness.

Take the example of a decommissioned billboard, its face now stripped blank, its framework removed to reveal an earlier hand-painted advertisement. Other than indicating a more evident history – that this prominent site has long been used for the purposes of advertising – the orientation of the revealed artefact may indicate a once clear line-of-sight from roads that no longer exist or viewing angles now obscured by neighbouring buildings.

In this way uncoverings can contribute to our understanding of architectural history apart from assisting with the reading of building styles, confused as they often are by the countless revivals and revisions.

But above all, uncoverings highlight the ephemeral nature of signage, advertising and corporate identity. Design is not just seen as part of our environment, but is part of us. This precarious lifespan reflects our own human anxieties of ageing, decline and demise.

Ironically, it is the very act of 'covering over' the previous signage that has enabled its preservation, shielding it from both the erosive effects of harsh climate and fickle revisions by owners. The original decision to conceal signage suggests that cultural significance was not given much consideration, let alone acknowledgement at the time. But with a broader public interest in signage, words and letters, we may see a time when some uncoverings will be considered worthy enough to be kept in view. In an age where signage is often the output from a digital file rather than hand-painted, future 'uncoverings' of current work appear less likely. The process of signage plays a part in this. Sign-writing (painting) directly onto a wall immediately bonds the artwork and wall surface together, whereas adhered vinyl or metal is more likely to be simply removed. This lends a greater sense of importance and appreciation to the uncoverings now being revealed.

Rumour has it

While most uncoverings are surprising to passers-by, others are known to be waiting for the day when they are once again revealed. The prominent façade of the Target department store in Bourke Street is said to conceal the original signage for Manton's, an old Melbourne emporium that was eventually transformed into a Coles Store. It will only be when the Target façade is one day peeled back that the additional layers will be brought back once again into public view.

A funny thing happened to me on the way

I was on my way to the Victoria Market one Sunday morning by tram, as my car had been broken down for some time. Going down Victoria Street, looking out the window, as you do, I noticed just briefly, for a split second, a sign that had never been there before. I thought, that's unusual – and it looked very old. So on the way back from the market I made sure I sat on that side of the tram with all my plastic bags. And I'm looking and looking as we're going along, and then there it was. Bang, in the middle of the window. Yet Sing Laundry. I thought 'A Chinese laundry sign. Wow!'. So I raced home, dumped all the plastic bags of food and rushed back down the street straight away.

When I got there, I saw that there were two Vietnamese guys up a ladder. Part of the sign was down already. I asked them what they were going to do with the sign. They said they were just going to take it to the tip, and I said, 'Well, do you mind if I have it?' They replied, 'No problem, you can have it. We cut it up for you!' I was horrified. 'No! Don't cut it up. Just take it down and put it on the ground and I'll take it away.' So I took what was already down and carried that home. When I came back there was a big pile of very long planks. And so I carried them one or two at a time all the way down Victoria Street through the traffic. Took three or four trips to do it.[1]

Dennis Bryans

to the market

OPPOSITE
Dennis Bryans with
the rescued Yet Sing
Laundry signage (1989)
*Photographer: Elisabeth
Disney. Image: Courtesy
of Dennis Bryans*

And so it was that good fortune (and a great deal of exuberance) played its part for Dennis Bryans, then a design lecturer at Swinburne University, in preserving a typographic artefact that richly speaks of the early Chinese migrant experience in Australia.

Originally installed in 1917 on the shop front of 349 Victoria Street in the inner-city suburb of Abbotsford, the Yet Sing Laundry sign was uncovered during renovations in 1989 when a false façade was removed.

Soon after Bryans salvaged the sign, he kindly donated it to the Melbourne Chinese Museum where it creates a striking display as an example of one of the many early mercantile opportunities for Chinese migrants in Australia.

The sign itself was painted by R. E. Boutcher, an English immigrant who established his signwriting business in Richmond in 1910. Known for his embellishments on carriages and suchlike, the Yet Sing Laundry sign was one of his first commissions in Australia.

The concealed modernist

Within the local community of late 1930s Werribee, the striking red Art Deco typographic titling of Callanan's Chemist symbolised more than just its location. It reflected a newly arrived and exciting modernity.

Designed by a Melbourne architect G. Simpson, the streamlined store façade promised the customer a new pharmacy experience, whereby 'the lightly coloured and brightly lit interior, the open display and striking signage were designed to attract customers and maximise sales'.[1] In Callanan's the customer could look into the dispensary, view the shelves of colourfully-packaged products and even have their baby weighed at a special counter. The graphics were eye-catching and completely integrated from inside to outside. These features all combined to express modern notions of progress in science, technology and efficient design.

The Callanan family business was finally sold in 2001. That same year Heritage Victoria formally recognised the significance of the chemist store. This process included the making of a film of the original shop environment,[2] as well as a full historical audit of the store. The completely intact original store design, as well as its complete uniqueness in the western region of Victoria, made the preservation of Callanan's extraordinarily important. But would the new owner have the same appreciation? It certainly appears so, for when the new owner, Pat Mount, decided to move the location of the chemist to ensure commercial viability, the entire fitout of the store was moved along with it.

The relocated store has since been sold. The displays and fitout of the original Callanan's Chemist no longer exist, although several items were saved and are now stored at the Werribee Historical Society offices (coincidently next door to the original store). The exterior Callanan's signage still exists on the original façade, preserved under a brutal metal hoarding.

Split identities

Many companies have been around so long that they feel the need to update their corporate identity. When those original identities are etched into concrete onto the factory façade some creativity is required to make the alterations. In other cases, a succession of updated signs can describe the journey of a business from its original beginnings to the present day.

The announcement of a new corporate identity can lead to a 'scorched earth' policy as staff scramble to erase all trace of the previous identity from their communications – business cards are shredded, signage is speedily torn down and cars are re-wrapped in vinyl.

Electronic communications have now made avoiding this collective shame of association with the 'old version' somewhat easier. Digital files can be erased or updated with the press of a button, leaving only remote shadows of the former self lingering on old servers and disconnected web links. But what did companies do when their corporate identity was etched into the façade of their buildings?

Sometimes companies just left the original name there, while others made curious modifications. With the forces of modernity arriving in the first half of the twentieth century, established companies saw a need to present a suitably progressive visual identity, communicating social and technological advancement. This saw the stripping away of any Victorian-era embellishment to be replaced by a cleaner, simplified modern public face.

Richmond's Rosella factory offers an interesting take on this. First registered as early as 1894, Rosella became a household name, perhaps best known for its sauces and jams. The origins of the company name Rosella have been open

to much speculation. It is said that in the early days of operation a large flock of Eastern Rosellas flew over their yard and so inspired the name. Another tale is that the name derives from the first names of the sisters or daughters of one of the founders, forming an amalgam of Rose and Ella. Either way, the branding of Rosella products has always featured the iconic bird in a myriad of different incarnations. To this very day the exterior walls of the extensive Rosella factory complex near the Yarra River display large sculpted depictions of the native Australian bird. However, closer observation of the Rosella signage reveals a little more.

At first glance the Rosella titling appears to be a simple sans serif font. But this is actually a later incarnation of the name. Company letterhead dating from the 1920s shows that the Rosella identity featured a linked sturdy script, embellished with an ornate keylined drop shadow. A sharp-eyed viewer will be able to see these forms actually sculpted on the factory façade. Committed to the built form of the original identity, the Rosella signage

its signage is more telling of the many lives the cinema has experienced over its lifetime. Across the one cinema many sets of signage incongruously exhibit their own particular vintage.

From the street the awning signage indicates the cinema's ownership by RMIT University, by way of their own corporate identity alongside a sympathetic 1920s-style sign bearing the name, Capitol Theatre. In complete contrast to this is a very heavy, condensed slab serif, set into the entranceway flooring, which many cinema-goers would regard as type ripped off from a 1950s Wild West film poster. Halfway up the stairs to the cinema patrons are welcomed by a widely expanded futuristic sans serif[1] in shiny golden metal, gesturing to the fantastical sci-fi type of the 1970s.

Despite this series of typographic time capsules, the original building signage can still be located. Echoing the complex sculptural forms of the Capitol ceiling, the original signage (located at a former rear cinema exit in Presgrave Place) features oddly exaggerated spiky wedge serifs. Perhaps intended to reflect the dense surrounding texture, these somewhat clumsy forms represent a dramatic departure from the clean and crisp modernist architectural titling common in the early twentieth century.

Harmonious or not, such diversity just within this one building does go some way to suggest the rich spectrum of typographic expression that exists within an ever-changing city.

was simply 'updated' by painting over the script linkages, giving the industrial complex a more streamlined, 'modern' appearance. It is a rare instance of signage presenting two identities at once – an odd adaption of the fancy ornament of the late 1800s towards a newer, functional modernity.

But Rosella is not alone in presenting many visual identities all at once. Although the interior design of the Capitol Theatre (1924), by the American architect Walter Burley Griffin and Marion Mahony, is considered a defining example of architectural modernity,

OPPOSITE
Paramount's Capitol Theatre, Melbourne (c. 1937–39) Commercial Photographic Co. negative, flexible base *Image: State Library of Victoria Pictures Collection* H2009.21/64

TOP LEFT
The 'Wild West' slab serifs of the Capitol Theatre foyer signage reflect its 1950s origins (2009) *Image: Author*

MIDDLE LEFT
Stairway signage at the Capitol Theatre displays the popularity of expanded (wide) sans serifs during the 1970s (2009) *Image: Author*

BOTTOM LEFT
With the purchase of the Capitol Theatre by RMIT, its identity is now merged wth that of the university (2009) *Image: Author*

TOP RIGHT
One of the original signs for the Capitol Theatre still exists but is well hidden down an alleyway (2009) *Image: Author*

Hidden within our streetscape are instances where signage design has been influenced by what is

Matching identities

...known as typographic onomatopoeia – when the name of the typeface matches the content itself.

Walking down the main street of South Melbourne, you may care to notice a strange occurance with the signage. The signs for Clarendon Street are designed in a typeface called (suitably) *Clarendon*.

At first this may come across as just an obscure joke, observed and understood only by graphic designers and typographers, but the relationship between place-name and typeface-name sets up a very specific visual identity to an area.

Type and place

There is certainly no shortage of typefaces whose names refer to their geographic point of origin or cultural influence (*Zurich*, *Chicago* and *Tarzana* just to name a few), so the connection between letters and a 'sense of place' is a well-established aspect of typography.

But typographic onomatopoeia turns this tradition on its head, giving an identity to a particular place through the (matching) typeface used.

The end result of this reversal is that our streetscape is, at least in a very small way, being influenced by the strangest and quietest of typographic connections.

'Our Magic Hour', it proclaims joyfully over the otherwise drab riverside industrial landscape of saw-tooth factory rooftops. As twilight fades, the happily rotund, rainbow-coloured neon letterforms spring to life, the sign's sense of joy amplified by its bright illumination. But its spirit of optimism is not without precedent.

Our magic times

This beacon of optimism sits oddly in the pragmatic factory landscape. Like the dramatic skysign signage it seeks to emulate, *Our Magic Hour* was built to be site-specific, but not for a site in Richmond, in fact not even in Melbourne.

Ugo Rondinone's striking installation was built by Kaldor Public Art Projects in 2003 to sit on top of the roofline of the Museum of Modern Art in Circular Quay, Sydney. The Swiss-born, New York-based artist exhibited the work as part of a major exhibition, after which it was brought to Melbourne, where it now sits on top of the headquarters of the Sportsgirl/Sussan fashion chain.

However, the act of moving artwork also moves its context, and with it, its meaning. The installation of *Our Magic Hour* in Melbourne opens up unintended interpretations and relationships within a wider history of the city's signage, branding and folklore.

The selection of the *Our Magic Hour* site could be seen as serendipitous. The art patron who generously brought this work to Melbourne, Naomi Milgrom, owns several fashion chains. According to Milgrom:

Placement of this work on the roof of our building is particularly appropriate because Richmond has such a well-established history of landmark signage, *with signs such as Skipping Girl Vinegar, Slade Knitwear, Nylex and Pelaco. Great care has been taken to reinforce the value and appreciation of existing heritage signs in the area.*[1]

While this newest addition to the Richmond skyline does indeed build upon the particularly dense cluster of signage, its new siting creates another completely unintended reference. The visual association between the joyously bright striping of *Our Magic Hour* and the well-established striped Sportsgirl branding creates a wonderfully flirtatious dual role for *Our Magic Hour* – as both contemporary art and as signage, the very visual language it has co-opted.

The optimistic spirit contained in the rainbow-coloured *Our Magic Hour* is not without precedent in Melbourne. If one walked down Bourke Street in the late 1800s one of the most striking features in the streetscape would undoubtedly have been the trademark rainbow signage above the entrance of the legendary Cole's Book Arcade. Owned and operated by the eccentric utopian Edward William Cole (1832–1918), the arcade was widely described as a 'palace to the intellect', overflowing with an assortment of new and secondhand books and other wares. However, the atmosphere was more akin to that of a circus – featuring a menagerie of animals, a fernery, distortive mirrors,

OPPOSITE
Our Magic Hour (2003)
Ugo Rondinone
neon, plexiglas,
translucent film, steel
(2011) *Image:*
Patrick Rodriguez

ABOVE
The renowned rainbow
of E.W. Cole from the 72nd
edition of *Cole's Funny
Picture Book*

PAGES 218 AND 219
The offices of John Wardle
Architects featuring the
neon installation *'and so
we say to the unborn,
watch out for life and ...'*
(2003)
Peter Kennedy
Image: Trevor Mein

a confectionery section and an assortment of curious machines and entertainments.

Cole's distinctive rainbow motif was also featured on the front of his best-selling, self-published *Cole's Funny Picture Book*, of which 400,000 copies found their way onto the bookshelves of Melbournians. When Cole's Book Arcade was finally pulled down in 1929, a decade after the founder's death, the cheery rainbow entranceway was sadly missed by many.

Although clearly unintended, the installation of *Our Magic Hour* over Richmond reflects that sense of public optimism that Cole had brought to the city more than 100 years previously.

High above Russell Street in the city glows an intriguing multi-coloured neon sentence – *'and so we say to the unborn, watch out for life and …'* A City of Melbourne public art project commissioned through John Wardle Architects, this piece by Melbourne artist Peter Kennedy was installed in 2003.

The statement itself, borrowed from Kurt Vonnegut's 1982 novel *Deadeye Dick*, was then modified to become

open-ended by the addition of an 'and …' on both ends, optimistically anticipating that the work might act as a starting point for a longer, ongoing conversation across the city. 'A continuous message onto other buildings. A narrative of a city.'[2] As Kennedy himself describes his relationship with typography; 'Within the context of text-based art, I try to differentiate my approach from other artists by using type and typography in a storytelling way'.[3]

The work spans the entire 36-metre length of the tenth floor of Total House. 'Laying it all out was really tricky, because it had to look like I wasn't compensating for the window frames. It had to look very natural. But there are minor adjustments in letter spacing.'[4]

The skills acquired during years spent working in the neon advertising industry have enabled Kennedy to explore this medium across many themes, particularly that of mortality.[5] Kennedy reflects on the Wardle commission:

We issue a kind of warning to watch out for life, because it can be fairly dangerous. However, one should not take all of this

too seriously. It can be viewed with a sense of humour. I don't want it to be regarded as a heavy or unduly profound statement, but even in whatever lightness it might have, the more you think about it the more profound it seems.[6]

Like *Our Magic Hour*, this work is situated on commercial premises occupied by its commissioners. Readily employing the familiar pop language of advertising, both works operate on two distinct levels: firstly, as working signage, in so much that they graphically indicate a specific location; and secondly at a more profound level, offering public statements of optimism, persuading passers-by to contemplate rather than consume.

The use of light is a deliberate and appropriate choice of media, literally and metaphorically illuminating a city. As a prominent figure in the art world, Chris McAuliffe, director of the Ian Potter Museum, commented at the switching on of *Our Magic Hour*, 'It has a message, but not the blunt message of an advertising sign. It's enigmatic and unfinished as a sentence'.[7]

CHARACTERS | 221

A new type of sporting identity

Partake in one of the most popular Australian pastimes – watching football – and you'll also be witnessing one of the most canny and technically advanced usage of logos and fonts in action.

Masterfully coordinated to the viewpoint of the various broadcast camera positions, the application of sponsor logos onto the grass surface of the field is distorted to compensate for natural perspective. So while the players appear as three-dimensional figures, the typography upon the field appears completely flat and therefore legible.

This process is known as 'anamorphic' signage. Although considered to be a relative new phenomen, the origins of the underlying principle date back to the sixteenth century.

Anamorphosis, the process of distorting an image to the point where it can only be seen clearly by the use of a mirror or similar device, was used not only in art[1] but also cleverly used to conceal political messages (and even early forms of pornography) within otherwise abstract images.

Artist Juan Ford employed this principle in his painting *Stretching the Truth* (2010) which depicts a lush green football field with the familiarly distorted logo stretched across it. Although the typographic language of the bold, bevelled and outlined sans serif capital letters is what we expect from a football logo, the name itself is less familiar.

The branding is in fact a ficticious logo for *marngrook*, an Aboriginal ball game originally played with a possum skin ball.

By projecting this invented signage across the field (of the Melbourne Cricket Ground, no less), Ford acknowledges the considerable influence this earlier Indigenous game has had on the formulation of Australian Rules Football and by association, an influence on a wider sense of place and community.

ABOVE
Stretching the Truth (2010)
Juan Ford
Oil on linen, 122 x 107 cms
Image: Courtesy of artist

In the background of the dimly lit, black-and-white scenes of apocalyptic Melbourne that appeared in the film *On The Beach* (1959), where the lack of petrol had caused people to revert to horse-drawn carriages while abandoned motor vehicles littered the streets, a curiously familiar landmark can be seen.

The huge painted signage for Mazda Lamps, spanning the entire width of a building, appears as a recognisable yet ghostly apparition.

Affectionately known as the 'Mazda Cat', its playful face is clearer, its cartoon features and associated typography more distinctive. More than half a century later the Mazda Cat is still there appearing in incidental glimpses in between the ever-growing verticality of the cityscape.

Often mistaken for its more famous Japanese motor vehicle namesake, Mazda Lamps had little to do with motoring. Mazda was, in fact, a trademark name created by the Shelby Electric Company in 1909 for its tungsten filament light bulbs.[1] The products, and indeed the company that made them, no longer exists. The Mazda Cat and everything it promoted are a legacy of a bygone era.

But exactly what legacy has the Mazda Cat left behind? What happens when an old sign eventually lags behind the ever-changing face of a city? Or when the business for which the sign was made moves location or no longer exists? The sign remains the same, perhaps sitting on top of a newly tenanted building, disconnected from its original purpose. Its voice, once bold and confident, becomes a shadow of a former time – of lost companies, products and services. Disconnected from its first life, it is now that something interesting happens.

Originally designed for advertising, these forms transcend their initial single purpose into an arguably more useful role – as a signifier of place and time. The connection they once had with a company is instead replaced by a public connection.

Instead of 'disconnected' signage simply being forgotten, it has in fact evolved, taking on a new life of its own. Viewers happily acknowledge that the original intended content no longer exists and instead read them as something quite different – as a familiar yet unique feature in their everyday lives.

In many cases the significance of signage as 'urban markers' is further reinforced by being all that remains of a place and time in the collective public memory. So perhaps instead of the Mazda Cat fading away from the cityscape, it may just be going through one of its many lives.

The many lives of 'Mazda Cat'

(Faux)nts of fancy

So seduced by technology were people in the early days of printing that it was said: 'If it's in print, it must be true'. A similar thing was even said of online information in its infancy. Even on our streets not every typographic environment you see is quite what it seems. Enter the phenomena of *(Faux)nts* – the false world of typography.

The White Mouse
(Opposite)
Near the Abbotsford Convent in inner-city Abbotsford, stands a small building, its signage written in French. A typographically ornate set, it was designed for the film *White Mouse* (1987), replicating a French country town under Nazi seige during the Second World War. The film tells the story of the New Zealand-born Nancy Wake (1912–), who fought in the French Resistance under the code name 'White Mouse'.

Although not an authentic feature of the 1863 Convent, the faux signage has now been embedded within the building's history by being protected by a strict heritage overlay whereby it cannot be altered or removed.

Considered by many to capture a European nostalgia and romance, the signage now has a second life – as one of the most popular backdrops for wedding photography in Melbourne.

Safari Toilet Block
(Overleaf)
Usually seen as a distant blur from the Western Highway, these remains are the last remaining relic of the Bullen's Lion Safari Park in Rockbank on the north-western outskirts of Melbourne.

Built in 1970 and cannily situated en route to the popular Ashton's Lion Park in Bacchus Marsh, the Bullen's Lion Park has long since closed, the only visible remnant being the walls of an old toilet block. Encroaching housing estates will eventually consume this extraordinary relic.

OPPOSITE
The mock Second World War signage preserved forever within the 1860s Abbotsford Convent (2011) *Image: Jesse Marlow*

PAGE 228–229
All that remains of the faux 'African Safari Lion Park', a lone toilet block out in the desolate fields of Rockbank (2011) *Image: Jesse Marlow*

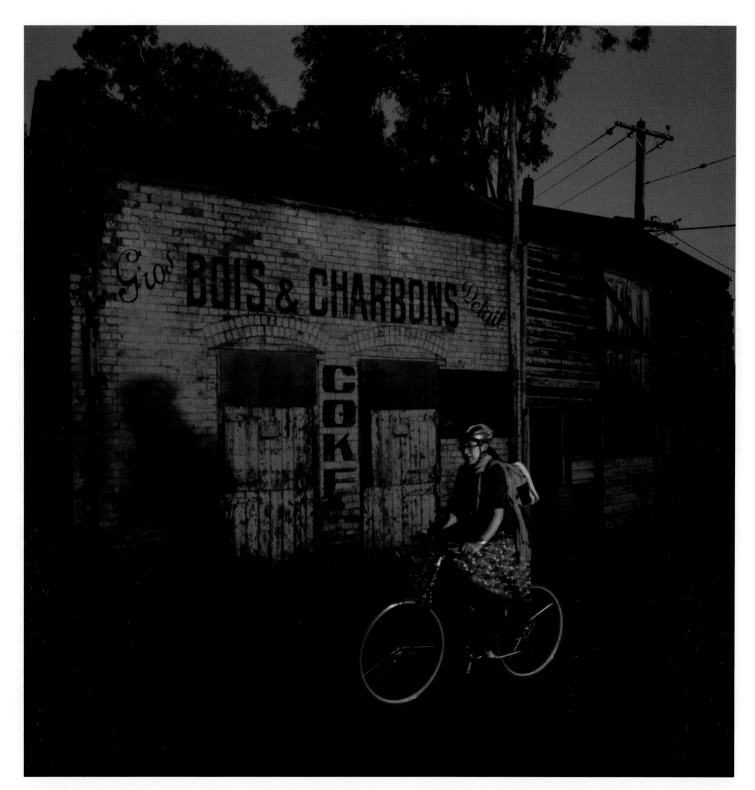

Once upon a time if you ran a fish and chip shop you would advertise its presence with a big plastic shark mounted on your roofline. Or if you sold ice creams you might have an ice cream cone up there. All that was required was a simple picture of your product. But in a newer age of diversification, what do you put on your roof if you sell fish, chips and ice creams?

The 27th letter of the alphabet

If your objective is visual impact, scaling an object to massive proportions usually does the trick. While the dramatic silhouette of this 'pictorial' signage is direct, immediate and eye-catching, it is really only useful for the communication of a single product. And so, until recently companies such as Bizz Buzz Hardware always had a very prominent street presence, compliments of the huge neon hammers that mark their locations.[1]

The literal depiction of a product was appropriate when businesses had a single message, but are now of limited use for the many abstract products and services that are common in the modern marketplace, such as branding services and intellectual property. These changes in the nature of businesses have necessitated a reappraisal of signage, causing it to develop into forms that are every bit as abstract as what they are communicating.

Increasingly, the visual language of signage is embracing a more sophisticated perspective through the use of abstract representation. This has expanded the definition of what is 'typographic' beyond the composition of letters. The night sky of Southbank features a huge red neon bracket – no words, no letters, just a brightly illuminated symbol.

It is not public art, nor is it a fragmented message from a damaged advertising sign – it is the external signage for the Melbourne Recital Centre. This huge red neon bracket points inwards to the building and derives from the Centre's corporate identity, a distinctive squarish silhouette made up of four such brackets. The abstraction has a dual purpose; for those familiar with the identity it readily identifies the location, and for others this directional device introduces them to the Centre's branding.

Designed in 2006, this outwardly-gesturing 'bracket' mark was developed to visualise aspects of the Centre's charter, particularly that of public inclusiveness. Its usage as a directional device in the external signage offers a logical extension of these virtues, as well as adding a unique feature to the Melbourne skyline.

OPPOSITE
The signage for Outboard Marine (OM) that once sat overlooking Sydney Road in Brunswick. It vanished soon after this photograph was taken (1998)
Image: Warren Kirk

Upsizing

The use of scale alone can transform a familiar form into a visual abstraction. The massive form of the Channel Seven logo in Melbourne's Docklands goes beyond just representing the location of the media organisation or as a visual representation of a single numeral. Its monstrous bright red folds become completely sculpturally abstract and could quite easily be mistaken for public art, particularly to those not familiar with the channel's brand. Its independent placement apart from any particular building or façade reinforces its power as a stand-alone artistic monument.

PAGES 232–233
The abstract street presence of the Melbourne Recital Centre (2011) *Image: Patrick Rodriguez*

OPPOSITE
Mentone Tenpin Bowling (c.1995) Warren Kirk *Image: Courtesy of State Library of Victoria Pictures Collection* H95.225/18

LEFT
The monumental numeral denoting the presence of Channel Seven in Melbourne's Docklands (2008) *Image: Tim Fluence Courtesy of Letterbox*

Absence

'You are here' the sign confidently exclaimed. This statement, set in bold type within a big black arrow was the lone feature of this city map. Surrounding it on all sides was a white void, all the streets, details and features long since completely sun-bleached into invisibility. So where exactly was here?

Erasure is part of city life. For some it may be described as renewal, for others its destruction. Whichever the perspective, this process has its own language, in fact, its own typographic language. These are the shadows of letters, words or statements long gone. And with their decommissioning is left its typographic legacy – paint or glue outlines of what was once there, what was once said.

But rather than falling silent, this 'language of erasure' offers an insight into more than just that specific business. In the case of failed large-scale commerce or decommissioned civic authorities it can contribute to a bigger story of the mercantile and political story of a city. Or it can be as simple as a way-finding sign pointing to a place that no longer exists.

Much of this phantom signage is easily legible through the good condition of the letter outlines. Others, such as logos, are recognisable, not through their individual letterforms but through a distinctive silhouette or colour. However, some have been degraded to a point of encryption, broken down into abstracted codes – blobs of glue scattered in a seemingly random fashion, like an aimless dot-to-dot game.

Unlike the typographic uncoverings (see page 204), obscured by subsequent layers of built form, these 'glue outlines' are the abandoned relics left behind to tell their story of demise, redundancy or simply relocation.

In terms of communication these letters operate by proxy, continuing their role of advertising or marking a (former) existence, while being viewed by a public with the benefit of hindsight. To the passer-by they invite speculation as to what happened – Did the organisation go bust? Was it bought out? Was it renamed or did it just move location?

In a society that fears personal or commercial failure, these curious marks left on building façades may be read by many as unsettling public reminders of someone's demise. In fact, these gluey traces communicate the perpetual and dynamic process of urban renewal – as one thing dies, another replaces it.

The number of these curious outlines in existence reflects the current state of our transient relationship with the corporate and civic structures around us. Whereas once authorities proudly displayed their permanence and reliability by having their titles cast in iron or artfully carved into their towering stone façades, a more ephemeral period is now serviced by materials such as perspex, plastic, vinyl and wafer-thin aluminium. These ghostly letterforms continue to tell us that nothing is forever – not even the mercantile foundations and governmental structures that were once thought of as unmovable.

Another, perhaps more obtuse aspect to absence is the phenomenon of un-signage. Instead of clearly marking a place, the proponents of un-signage deliberately presume a familiarity of a place. A popular joke relating to Melbourne bars is that many celebrate the 'less signage, more hip' approach. This complete absence of conventional forms of recognition reinforces an unwritten sub-cultural code, roughly translated as 'if you can't find us we wouldn't let you in anyway'.

One memorable instance of encoded signage was the discrete projection of a tiny logo onto a doorway – down a laneway and visible only at night. Given its intentional ambiguity, it could either excite, baffle, intimidate or simply tell you that you have reached your destination.

PAGES 236–237
Glue outlines of signage
(2011) Warren Kirk
Image: Courtesy of artist

PAGES 240–241
Smith's Crisps factory
(c.1940–1949)
Lyle Fowler
negative, flexible base
*Image: State Library of
Victoria Pictures Collection*
H92.20/708

OPPOSITE
The shadowy traces
of various signs now
removed (c. 1991–2005)
Image: Author

PAGES 242–243
Hume Highway Project
(2010)
Peter Atkins
*Image: Courtesy of artist
and Tolarno Galleries*

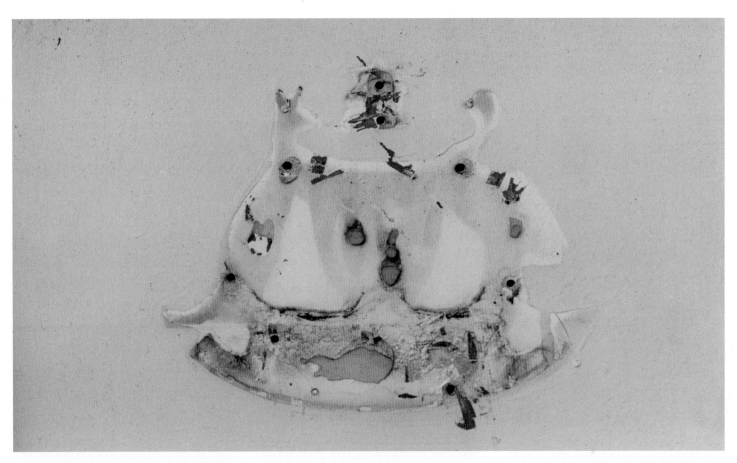

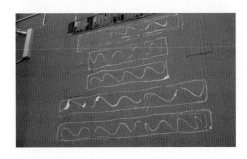

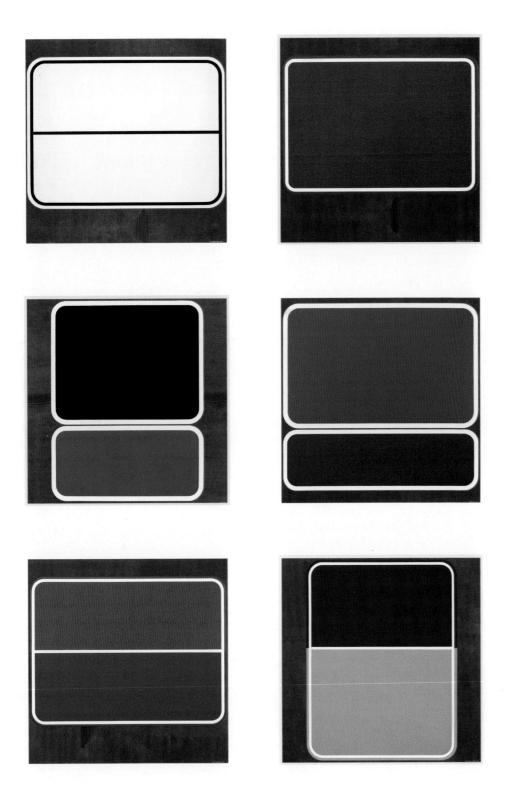

For artist Peter Atkins, our complete familiarity with the visual language of highway signage is used to introduce other meanings to their representation – with a complete absence of typography. The *Hume Highway Project* (2010) is a series of bold colour blocks framed with the familiar rounded edges of 'highway language', as Atkins terms it.

> *I have photographed hundreds of signs along the highway in both directions from Melbourne to Sydney and back again. It was only later, after I had begun this documentation process, that I could look beyond these signs, past their words and see them differently from their intended purpose. I had begun to see these signs as simply beautiful abstract forms.*[1]

Designed for distance reading, the role of colour in highway signage is central to their legibility. Each colour combination communicates different content: green with white type indicates directions, distances and places; brown with white type is used for cultural destinations; blue signs are for petrol, food and rest areas; while red with white type carries the immediacy of safety information and warnings.

But it is the absence of typography, and all the site-specific information this would bring, that makes these works resonate in a purely symbolic sense. Although Atkins' *Hume Highway Project* focuses on a rural experience, his sharp observations highlight the capacity for signage (even without text) to operate both as markers for geographic sites, as well as a framework for our own individual mapping of space.

NEW HOMES: Your guide to the best
new homes, developers and home renovations.
INSIDE **DOMAIN TOMORROW**

Museum and designer see red

government order to remove

By **DAVID ROOD**
STATE POLITICAL REPORTER

AN ORDER by the Brumby Government to remove the City Museum's sculptured red signs, worth $110,000, from outside the Old Treasury Building has sparked outrage, with claims it will seal the museum's fate.

Tourism Minister Tim Holding directed that the signs, which were partly funded by the former Bracks government, be taken away as they were "totally inconsistent" with the heritage value of the building.

But the museum and the designer of the signs, academic Garry Emery, argue they are totally in keeping with the history of the Spring Street building, completed in 1862, and have heritage approval.

In a letter to Mr Holding, Mr Emery said the use of contemporary design on historical buildings had been successfully employed overseas. "The pyramid entry to the Louvre Museum or the Ministry of Culture in Paris, the dome on the Reichstag in Berlin ... are some examples of this," he wrote. "This approach reflects the necessity of adapting historical buildings to a current and relative role. The best way of preserving historical buildings is to use them."

Mr Emery said the building was originally constructed to discourage people from entering, and the signs were designed to guide people into the museum.

The red signs sit across the steps of the Old Treasury building that once stored gold bullion; they were funded by the museum and a $40,000 contribution from the Victorian Government.

Museum director Jo-Anne Cooper said the museum signs, installed in 2005, had increased visits by 30% and were used in the museum's tourism and information brochures.

Ms Cooper said she first heard of the decision to take away the signs on Wednesday in an email from a government department, and their removal "clearly spells the demise of the museum".

"The lack of consultation was

The Reichstag's dome in Berlin, and the Louvre's glass pyramid in Paris.

The large, angular red "City Museum" sign outside the Old Treasury Building is under a government removal order.   PICTURE: GEORGINA PAPAGIANNIS

Heritage not so bold

There's nothing like signage to evoke a battle between the forces of old and new; between heritage and change. The public response to these striking structures can range from spirited campaigns for their protection (as seen in the cases of Skipping Girl, Pelaco and Slade Knitwear) through to vitriolic accusations of vandalisation and pollution of the public environment. Such intensity is particularly amplified when the signage in question is placed on, or near, places of perceived historical significance.

Keeping heritage alive

The most prominent of these has been the dispute over the signage for the Melbourne City Museum at the Treasury Building. The external signage, designed by Gary Emery and installed in 2005, consisted of bright red angular planes sculpturally folded around the stairs of the landmark Spring Street building. In July 2008 the Victorian State Government saw fit to order the removal of the signage, claiming that it was 'totally inconsistent' with the heritage value of the 1862 building.

Both the designer and the City Museum director Jo-Anne Cooper defended the heritage-approved signage. Mr Emery spoke of the importance of signage bringing people inwards to use the space: 'The best way of preserving buildings is to use them'.[1] Estimating that the signage had increased city museum visits by 30 per cent, Ms Cooper speculated that its removal 'clearly spells the demise of the museum'.[2]

In January 2010 the City Museum closed its doors. For a period of time Emery's signage sat out on the stairway, gesturing to a place that no longer existed. It too has now been removed.

Cleaning up the neighbourhood

The design and installation of the landmark signage for the Arts House, North Melbourne Town Hall, required a long process of community consultation, particularly with heritage groups who strongly opposed it in the early stages. As it turns out, the signage may have provided some social good as well as navigation. To accommodate the Queensberry Street signage a long bank of public telephone boxes had to be removed, leading to a pertinent comment, by Jim Cathcart, the director of the Arts House at the time of installation, 'Overnight this signage has probably halved North Melbourne's drug deals'.

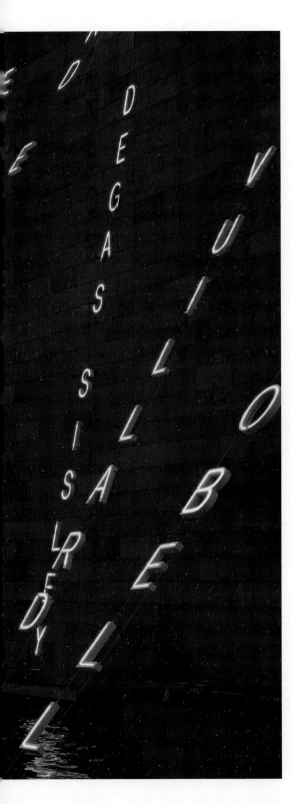

The fine threads of art

In 2010 the National Gallery of Victoria featured an eye-catching typographic display at the main entrance to their St Kilda Road building to advertise the *European Masters* exhibition held there as part of *Melbourne Winter Masterpieces* series. Employing LED illumination, the long threads of letters appeared to float in mid-air, each thread spelling out the names of one or more artists whose works appeared in the exhibition.

ANZ

PRICEWATERHOUSE

adaps

ISIS

RYDGES

PORSCHE

STAMFORD

POST

st.geor

SOFITEL

Logo constellation

Stargazers often complain that the brightness of our cities causes 'light pollution' across the night skies, making it harder for stars to be clearly seen. There is another dimension to this – that the city itself has its own nocturnal constellation – signage.

Stargazers vs Mayne

As the architectural details of the city softly fade into darkness, an entire constellation of words and shapes begin to emerge out of the inky night sky. The night sky of signage is a dynamic one. One can use it to gauge whether the city is experiencing a building boom by counting the number of brightly illuminated, angled words visible across the city.

Set upon towering cranes that seem to float invisibly above the city, the words take on an abstract sense. Seen as a series of words, one can't help but want to put them together to form some sort of a narrative – the endless story of a city's perpetual construction and demolition, decay and renewal. The sky is scattered with illuminated abstractions, each dot of light taking the shape of a letterform, a shape or something else difficult to recognise. Words and logos are randomly dissected by the odd dysfunctional globe or tube.

In 2002 a controversy arose over one of these 'stars' being just a little too bright. A 7.5 metre-wide bright red Mayne neon sign, erected on St Kilda Road, was getting in the way of the astronomers working at the Old Melbourne Observatory. According to the Astronomical Society of Victoria, the neon light created by the Mayne logo created a foggy glow, blotting out the sky behind it.

Barry Clark, the society's director of Outdoor Light Improvement, noted:

The sign looks twice the size of the full moon – and is brighter. It's the second-brightest thing in the sky after the sun. If we're looking in a southerly direction, we've got this blasted sign lighting up the sky. The things we're looking at – the stars, the galaxies, clouds of gas and space – are about 30,000 times fainter than the sign itself.[1]

The permit for the huge neon sign, a large red circle with the word 'Mayne' written across its centre, was intended to be featured on the north, south and east sides of the building. Protests from local residents concerning the strength of the red glow saw the sign on the south side turned off.

Despite this, the debate uncovered the distinct lack of legislation regarding the issue of 'light pollution'.

So it appears that for the time being our city skies will continue their nightly show, brightly displaying their own odd but beautiful flickering collection of stars.

PAGES 248–249
The urban constellation of illuminated logos and titling. *Image: Patrick Rodriguez*

OPPOSITE
A digital recreation of the Mayne neon sign (without titling) which caused offence amongst war veterans due to its similarity to the Japanese flag. *Image: Letterbox*

Shrine vs Mayne

It wasn't just the brightness of the Mayne signage that had parts of the community up in arms. The glowing red circle of the Mayne logo floating high above the Melbourne Shrine of Remembrance brought with it another set of protests – this time due to the symbolism of the signage.

Former Prisoners of War complained to Shrine trustees that the neon sign 'looks like the Rising sun'. Shrine Trustees chief executive, Dennis Baguley said that the sign posed a threat to one of Melbourne's most treasured monuments. 'Because it is a big red circle it could be construed to be a Japanese flag'.

The Shrine Trustees wrote to Mayne requesting that the neon sign be permanently turned off. The company refused on the grounds that they had met all requirements in applying for the permit and that any protests should have been lodged during this process.

For Bill Toon, a former inmate of Singapore's notorious Changi Prison, the sign detracted from the Shrine:

'After returning home from being Prisoners of War we had somewhere to go and think of all the people who didn't return. This company [Mayne] is showing no reverance for the people who lost their lives. The sign brings back a lot of bad memories.[2]

The Mayne neon sign was removed in April 2006.

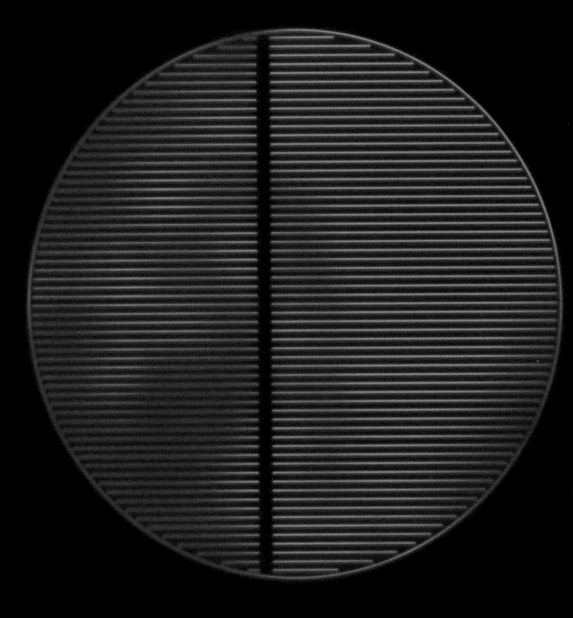

Finders keepers:

THE LOST MUSIC

The world of signage can lead to all sorts of curious discoveries.

One day I had to go and inspect the huge Sitmar Cruises neon at the end of Elizabeth Street on Flinders Street Station. It was about 50 foot long (15 metres) and displayed three different messages, including a great big ship revolving around. It had blown a fuse, and I thought, 'Oh bugger, where's the fuse for this thing?' Because, of course, the railways had bloody switchboards all over the place. So I got on up on the roof. I was walking along the roof following this conduit to one of those little beehives along the side of the railway building. There was an old rusty lock on the thing. I just ripped it off with my screwdriver and I went in. There was a little trapdoor up in the roof and the bloody conduit went up into that and I thought, 'You bastard!'. So I had to go downstairs and get a big pair of steps and drag it up. Got them into the bloody thing, got up, pushed the trapdoor open and stuck my head in.

'There was about 100 musical instruments in there. All beautiful silver trumpets and trombones, violins, guitars, banjos. All the glue had come undone and they'd fallen into a heap of three-ply on the floor and all the skins had gone off the drums. And I thought, 'What a strange f***ing thing this is.' So I went down to the man in grey and asked if he had ever lost anything here. [It turned out] the bloke who hid them up there was told to hide the instruments because at the start of the Second World War everybody thought the Japs [the Japanese] were coming. He built a false ceiling in and put all the stuff up there and closed it up. He belonged to the Salvation Army band in Brunswick and they all went away with the Second 21st Australian Brigade to Singapore.

'They were all captured by the Japs. As they were getting taken to Japan for forced labour, the troop ship they were on was torpedoed by a Yanky [US] ship. They were locked down in the hold. Two thousand of them went to the 'bottom bank' – one of the biggest Australian losses of life in the War. And he was the bloke that hid them; he'd worked for the railways.

'They searched everywhere for these instruments – in Flinders Street, Spencer Street – couldn't find them. And so I said to the man in grey, 'Well, I think I've just found them'. Apparently after the Second World War there was a reward of 100 quid for finding them. Well I said, 'I'll expect a cheque'. And I'm still waiting …'[1]

Ian 'Podgy' Rogers | NEON MAINTENANCE MAN

Finders keepers:

THE LOST WINGS

One time we were at the Essendon Aerodrome putting up these huge 8 foot (2.5 metre) tubes up in the main hangar. So there we were, out on this scaffold and we reached the roof. I could see a set of wings, a set of wheels, the engine and the body of an aeroplane, and I thought, 'What a bloody funny thing to leave up on a roof'.

'And I got down and told them that I had to bang a scaffold up against [their] building and then I asked, 'What have you got the aeroplane up there for?' He said, 'We haven't got an aeroplane up there. How would you fit a big aeroplane up there?' I said, 'Not a big aeroplane. It's a bloody Tiger Moth and it's got TAA written on it.

'So I got him up the ladder and he looked over and he said 'That's it!' Turned out that it had been missing for years and years. They'd put the plane up there as a promotion and then covered it up with another sign at the front saying 'Fly TAA, the friendly way'. Eventually nobody remembered it was there.

'Years later I was telling this story to an old lady who had been one of Australia's first commercial pilots. She said 'You're kidding – we flew thousands of miles looking for that aeroplane. That was TAA's first plane, the Tiger Moth. We flew all over Australia, up through the islands, we did all the bush airports. Couldn't find the bloody thing. They said it must have crashed somewhere in the bush!'[2]

Ian 'Podgy' Rogers | NEON MAINTENANCE MAN

The many lives of Astoria

For rare signage to be saved once is to be truly celebrated. For it to be saved from destruction twice is nothing short of a miracle. Such is the story of the neon script of Astoria Taxis.

Astoria Taxis was established in 1950 by the Gange family, a taxi dynasty dating back to the 1860s. To mark their Swanston Street presence a huge neon sign was erected on top of their Carlton headquarters in 1950.

This huge bright script that spelt out 'Astoria Taxis' had been masterfully designed, manufactured and lit by Whiteway. The installers of this sturdy yet elegant metal type even proudly painted their signatures ('Fred and Joe 1950') on the back of the 'T', the tallest of the letters, standing some 1.8 metres tall and 15 cm wide. And there it proudly stood for nearly 50 years lighting up the Carlton skyline with a warm and distinctive red glow.

In 2000 the taxi company decided to move its headquarters and in the process develop the now very valuable Swanston Street real estate into apartments. The day before the wrecking ball was set to demolish the blonde brick Art Deco building, along with its emblematic neon script, one member of the Gange family decided something had to be done to save the signage. Kevin M. Gange, grandson

of the original Astoria founder, saw that an important symbol of the taxi dynasty was about to be lost to the scrap metal yard. 'We certainly won't be throwing it out. Absolutely not. It's part of the heritage of the family. It's a work of art.'[1]

He managed to organise a small group of labourers to climb up to the roof, unbolt the signage and remove the massive script letter by letter. The next day the building fell but the signage survived, safely stored away in the taxi workshops of the new headquarters. The saved Astoria signage was to be

part of Kevin's grand plan to house a taxi museum at the new Rupert Street Collingwood headquarters. But fate had another plan. Early in the morning of 28 July 2009, a fire quickly spread throughout the entire Silver Top Building.[2] 'The heat of the fire was extraordinary – it burnt everything, melted metal down to nothing,' Gange reflected on that tragic night. The taxi museum with its collection of old vehicles was almost completely destroyed, even reducing an original 1860 handsome cab to nothing more than

a pile of ash and a warped metal frame. Amidst the roaring flames and scorching cinders, the firemen managed to hurriedly roll out some vehicles and drag out some of the contents of the workshops. As it turns out, this included the letters of the Astoria Signage.

Although slightly singed and blackened from the fire, the sculptural script sits intact awaiting the second incarnation of the Gange Taxi Museum. Its eventual inclusion will lead to a full restoration of its metal casing and replacement of the neon tubing.

One of only two remaining script neon skysigns in Melbourne (the other being Slade Knitwear, see page 140), the Astoria signage owes its 60-year vintage to two very dramatic survivals.

PAGE 256
The Astoria sign on top of its original Swanston Street building position (1994)
Warren Kirk
Image: Courtesy of artist

PAGE 257
Signatures of the original sign painters 'Fred and Joe' (2010)
Image: Tim Fluence

PAGES 258–259
The slightly scorched Astoria sign awaiting its reinstatement in the Gange Taxi Museum (2010) *Image: Tim Fluence*

OPPOSITE
Detail of the Astoria sign (2010) *Image: Tim Fluence*

ABOVE
The second half of the Astoria sign (2010)
Image: Tim Fluence

Endnotes

LEARNING TO SPELL

1 *emelbourne: The City Past and Present*, 'My Melbourne: childhood memories' by Dame Phyllis Frost at http://www.emelbourne.net.au/ biogs/EM01119b.htm Viewed 13 April 2011.

WHO WE ARE, LETTER BY LETTER

1 There are two main types of typefaces – serif and sans serif. Serif fonts have a small extension attached to the main stroke of the letterform, and are generally used for text as they are easier to read. Sans serif fonts have no extensions and are generally used for posters, signs and headings.

2 Typo website at www.typoshop.com.au Viewed 11 April 2011.

3 Interview with Natasha Skunca, 6 January 2011.

4 M. Harden, 'Review: Joe's Shoe Store', *The Age*, 3 December 2007.

5 Andres Janser and Felix Studinka, *Typotecture: Typography as Architectural Imagery*, Lars Muller Publishers, 2002, p. 5

6 ibid.

7 ibid.

8 ibid., p. 37.

9 Interview with Michelle Hamer, 27 January 2011.

10 ibid.

11 Interview with Jon Campbell, 11 February 2011.

12 ibid.

13 ibid.

14 Interview with Corbett Lyon, 9 January 2011.

15 Jock Kenneir, *Words and Buildings; The Art and Practice of Public Lettering*, The Architectural Press, London, 1980, p. 188.

LOOKING INWARDS

1 *emelbourne: The City Past and Present*, http://www.emelbourne.net.au/biogs/EM01734b. htm Cultural Heritage Unit. Viewed 13 April 2011.

2 *Transition*, Nº 22/23. *Reviews: Re-presenting the City: Cocks, Carmichael, Whitford's CentreWay Arcade*, Collins Street, Melbourne 1984–1987. Department of Architecture, RMIT, Summer 1987.

A PUBLIC SCANDAL

1 Based on an inspection of the premises at 98 Errol Street, North Melbourne, 27 March 2010.

AQUA PROFONDA

1 Victorian Heritage Document H1687, http://www.onmydoorstep.com.au/heritage-listing/4742/aqua-profonda-sign-fitzroy-pool

2 Helen Garner, *Monkey Grip*, Penguin, Camberwell, 2008.

3 *Aqua Profonda* was the name of a local school musical featuring children from North Fitzroy Primary School. Produced by Michael Cathcart and Hannie Rayson.

FIRE BRANDING

1 Eve Sainsbury, 'A Mark of Protection'. Exhibition label for *The Changing Face of Victoria*, State Library of Victoria, Jan–Dec 2011.

P FOR POST, T FOR TELEPHONES

1 GFC – Gas and Fuel Corporation; MMBW – Melbourne and Metropolitan Board of Works; MCCESB – Melbourne City Council Electricity Supply Board; PMG – Post Master General.

2 O. Harvey, 'The man who markets images', *Courier Mail* (Brisbane), 17 July 1982, p. 21.

THE WHITE CITY

1 T. Fry, *Design History Australia*, Hale & Iremonger and the Power Institute of Fine Arts, 1988.

2 *Australian Dictionary of Biography* – Online edition at http://adbonline.anu.edu.au/biogs/A110427b.htm

3 ibid.

4 J. Robertson, *MacRobertson the Chocolate King*, Lothian Books, 2004, p. 32.

5 Fry, op. cit., 1988.

6 M. Robertson, *A Young Man and a Nail Can: An industrial romance*, Melbourne, Specialty Press, 1921.

7 'Large electrical sign in Melbourne', *Australasian Electrical Times*, 27 July 1922. p. 387.

8 Robertson, op cit. 1921.

THE KING OF CARLTON

1 Thank you to Paolo Baracchi from the Italian Historical Society for this information.

THE GLOWING PARK

1 Interview with Leanne O'Shea, 25 May 2011.

POOLSIDE

1 The typeface used in the Lindrum signage is *Base 9* (Bold, small caps), designed by Zuzana Licko in 1995 and released by the Californian type foundry Emigré.

2 Although the building was often named after its initial owners, Griffiths Tea, it was also called 'Gravure House' in the 1960s after the various Herald subsidiary publications and companies, including *Colorgravure Publications*, United Press and *Home Beautiful*. The photograph of the eastern side of the Griffiths Tea Building was taken by Geoff Hocking prior to it being 'entombed' by an adjacent building.

THE CAGED KANGAROO

1 John Ford, The One Centre, in S. Canning & S. Creedy, 'Designers hopping mad over change of logo,' *The Australian*, 24 July 2007.

SPAGHETTI TYPE

1 Heritage Alliance, *Historic Electric Signage in Victoria. A Study of Historic Illuminated Signs*, August 2001, p. 9.

CHEERS TO THE THREE GLASSES

1 R. Annear, *A City Lost And Found*, Black Inc. Publishing, p. 189.

2 R. Beck, 'The art of Richard Beck', *Architecture and Arts*, Issue 39, November 1956.

3 *Design World*, Nº 25. 1992, pp. 4, 5.

FROZEN IN TYPE

1 emelbourne.net.au, Cultural Heritage Unit, University of Melbourne.

THE CHANGING LIGHTS AT THE CHANGING LIGHTS

1 Written correspondence between Jenny Elphingstone and City of Port Phillip, 2 September 1996.

2 Interview with Nevin Phillips, 20 December 2010.

3 National Trust database at http://vhd.heritage.vic. gov.au/search/nattrust_result_detail/66440

SPEED READING

1 'The cars that ate Melbourne', *The Age Review*, 14 February 2004.

2 R. Boyd, *The Australian Ugliness*, Penguin, 1957.

3 National Trust (Victoria) Media Release, 23 January 2009.

SIMPLE SAM

1 Interview with David Kilderry, 3 January 2011.

AT THE INTERSECTION OF TOPOGRAPHY AND TYPOGRAPHY

1 *Shell House Journal*, April 1958, p. 17.

2 *Heritage Electric Signs in Victoria*. Heritage Alliance, August 2001, p. 7.

3 *Shell House Journal*, op. cit.

4 Interview with Nevin Phillips, Delta Neon, 16 December 2010.

5 *The Age, Reflections: 150 Years of History*, Transworld Publishers, 2004, p. 152.

SPINNING A TALE OF SIGNAGE

1 Interview with Nevin Phillips, 20 December 2011.

BEACON OF THE WEST

1 The neon quartet comprises the Pelaco, Slade Knitwear, Nylex and Skipping Girl signs.

2 'Fenner lights up history', *International Longwall News*, 1 July 2002.

3 Tim Noisette, 'A sign of the times gets a welcome facelift', *Western Times*, n.d.

4 ibid.

5 The targeting of signage by shooters is not uncommon. The Dimmeys Emporium globe in Richmond (see page 172) also features several bullet holes. It was speculated that the attractive sphere was used as target practice by local constabulary in early Melbourne.

ALL LIT UP AND NOWHERE TO GO

1 OAAA, *Outdoor Advertising Association of Australia Report*, 1975.

2 The Holden sign was considered to be the largest neon sign in Australia at the time. Each letter was 7.5 metres tall.

3 T. Thwaites, 'City lights', *The Age Weekender*, 5 February 1982, p. 10.

4 A. Attwood, 'In Melbourne: Signs of the times', *Time Magazine*, 4 September 1986, p. 3.

5 A. Attwood, 'New hope for an old landmark', *The Age*, 16 March 1987.

6 Letter from Claude Neon Sales Manager, Warren Gleeson, to Advertising Manager at Allen's Sweets, Jack Wheat, 17 July 1968.

7 Letter from Evan Walker, Minister of Planning and Environment Victoria to Bill Isaacs, Allen's Sweets, 24 September 1985.

8 A. Attwood, op.cit.,

9 B. Millington, 'Sweetness and light', *The Age*, 17 March 1987.

10 ibid.

11 D. Miller, 'Lecturer looks at a sweet new way to brighten RMIT', *Herald*, 17 March 1987.

12 A. Attwood, op.cit., *Time Magazine*, 1986, pp. 3-4.

13 ibid.

14 Interview with Rick Charylo, Able Excavations and Demolitions, 16 September 2010.

WRITTEN BY THE HAND OF A GIANT

1 'A dim outlook for neon lights', *The Age*, 27 June 2001.

2 K. Heinrich, 'Is neon Melbourne on the blink?' *The Age*, n.d.

3 Residents in a Neon Glow (RING) submission to Heritage Victoria. RC 50.1 Slade Knitwear Sign. p. 3, The only other example of a cursive script is the Astoria Taxi sign.

4 *The Age*, op. cit., 27 June 2001.

5 Interview with Craig Rossetti, 8 February 2011.

GET SHIRTY

1 'Sunday Life', *Sunday Age*, Cover, 23 July 2000.

6.38

1 Expert Witness Report for Registrations Committee of the Heritage Council. Andrew Ward, Architectural Historian.

2 National Trust of Australia (Victoria) *Classification Report, Nylex Sign*, FN 7130.

3 Interview with Ian (Podgie) Rogers, 30 December 2010.

4 F. Hudson, 'Let there be light', *Herald Sun*, 1 January 2010.

LITTLE AUDREY

1 Interview with Ian (Podgie) Rogers, 30 December 2010.

2 Whelan the Wrecker had an office and a wrecking yard in Brunswick, named the Stawell Buildings, where Humphries found the original Audrey. The site has now been developed into apartments, but the Sydney Road façade remains.

3 John Mangan, 'Apostles, Luna Park, trams ascend pedestal', *The Age*, 4 November 2007.

4 Interview with Ian (Podgie) Rogers, 30 December 2010.

THE 'OTHER' GIRL

1 C. Webb. 'She lit up lives, but Skating Girl was all ice', *The Age*, 27 March 2009.

2 St Kilda Historical Society, 'St Moritz - The Skating Lady', at http://www.skhs.org.au/~SKHSarticles1/articles/St_Moritz.html

3 ibid.

4 It was taken out of storage temporarily for the exhibition *Signs of the Times* at the City Museum, Melbourne in 2005-07.

NEON GIRL TRIO

1 Based on notes by Patricia Hocking of an interview with Trevor Craddock from the State Savings Bank in 1972.

NAKED, YOUNG AND JACKSON

1 K. Dunstan, 'Moi? A distraction? Never, Monsieur', *Herald Sun*, 16 February 1989.

2 C. Lucas, 'Neon signs plan for mall', *The Age*, 31 January 2007.

3 Planning Committee Report, 5 February 2008. *Young and Jackson Hotel (Application Nº TP-2007-984)*. Agenda Item 5.5

4 L. Sinclair, 'Young and Jackson Hotel topped by lucrative billboard', *The Australian*, 1 September 2008.

SHE'S CRAVIN' ME

1 Interview with Ian (Podgey) Rogers, 30 December 2011.

ART OR BILLBOARD?

1 N. Draffin, *The Art of Napier Waller*, Sun Academy Series, 1978.

WHAT'S THE TIME? IT'S A B PAST AN M ...

1 S. Furphy, *Dimmeys of Richmond, The Rise and Fall of a Family Business*. Hyland House, 2007.

2 ibid.

TYPOTECTURE

1 Correspondence with Neil Masterton, 25 March 2011.

2 ibid.

3 Interview with Paul Hede, Hede Architects, 11 January 2011.

4 ibid.

5 P. Baines and C. Dixon, *Signs, Lettering in the Environment*, Laurence King Publishing, London, 2003, p. 101.

6 It is a geographic oddity that the western suburbs of Melbourne feature a number of architectural and signage references to 'Rising Sun' symbolism (The Sun Theatre, Rising Sun Hotel, and so on), when the sun actually rises in the east. In fact, this indicates the popularity of the 'rising sun' as a nationalist, empiric motif in working-class areas. The motif was devised in 1904 for Australian soldiers during the Boer War.

7 Interview with Ian McDougall, ARM, 25 March 2011.

THE BIG STEAL

1 All efforts to re-contact NTA Signs for further details were unsuccessful. The information provided was based on a phone interview with NTA Signs in 2005.

PEELING THE ONION

1 A further note from John Denton from DCM mentions that the 'panels, planes, sticks and constructions in vibrant blue, green, yellow, orange and red overlaid on the natural grey render tones' on the Adelphi Hotel become a form of 'sign'.

A FUNNY THING HAPPENED ...

1 Interview with Dennis Bryans, 18 September 2010.

THE CONCEALED MODERNIST

1 K. Webber and I. Hoskins. *What's in Store. A History of Retailing in Australia*. Powerhouse Publishing, Sydney, 2003.

2 *Callanan's Pharmacy, Past to Present*. DVD (6 mins), FL video.

SPLIT IDENTITIES

1 The font is *Microgamma* (1952, Aldo Novarese), used extensively in 1970s science fiction, particularly the *Star Trek* series.

OUR MAGIC TIMES

1 Correspondence with Naomi Milgrim, 25 May 2011.

2 Interview with Peter Kennedy, 14 December 2010.

3 ibid.

4 ibid.

5 Kennedy worked at the Sydney Office of Claude Neon from 1967 to 1972.

6 Interview with Peter Kennedy, 14 December 2010.

7 G. Coslovich, 'Bright lights, Big concept', *The Age*, 31 July 2003.

A NEW TYPE OF SPORTING IDENTITY

1 Interview with Juan Ford, 29 December 2010.

THE MANY LIVES OF 'MAZDA CAT'

1 The name was bought by General Electric in 1914 and used until 1945. The company chose the name due to its association with [Ahura] Mazda, the transcendental and universal God of Zoroastrianism whose name means '[Wise] Lord ' in the Avestan language.

THE 27TH LETTER OF THE ALPHABET

1 There is only one Bizz Buzz Hardware neon hammer left in existence. This is located in Thornbury, but the hardware store it sits on has now closed. There are plans to preserve the signage.

ABSENCE

1 Interview with Peter Aktins, 22 February 2011.

HERITAGE NOT SO BOLD

1 D. Rood. Museum and designer see red over government order to remove sign, *The Age*, 25 July 2008.

2 ibid.

3 Personal communication with Jim Cathcart, 2008.

LOGO CONSTELLATION

1 F. Tomazin, 'Stargazers take dim view of night sky', *The Age*, 22 May 2002.

2 P. O'Neil, 'War veterans see red', *Herald Sun*, 22 June 2004, p. 13

FINDERS KEEPERS

1 Interview with Ian (Podgey) Rogers, 30 December 2010.

2 ibid.

THE MANY LIVES OF ASTORIA

1 Interview with Kevin Gange, 12 April 2010.

2 'Trip the light fantastic', *Melbourne Leader*, c. August 2009.

Acknowledgements

This book would not have been possible without the generous assistance of many individuals and organisations.

If it were not for the potential imagined by the commissioning editor at Thames and Hudson Australia, Paulina de Laveaux, this book may well have remained just an idea.

The careful editing of these 272 pages by Margaret Trudgeon is also very much appreciated, making sense of words written by somebody who was at times just a little too close to the subject.

The enormous support of the State Library of Victoria in co-publishing this book has allowed access to and use of their extensive and diverse collections. I wish to thank Shane Carmody, Robert Heather and Shelley Roberts for seeing virtue in such a project. Thank you also to others within the library for their direct assistance: Margot Jones (Publishing); Eve Sainsbury, Emma Bloom (Exhibitions); Des Cowley (Rare Books); Madeleine Say, Gerard Hayes, Bridie Flynn, Mike Thomas (Pictures) and Peter Mappin (Imaging).

Parts of the research and production stages of this book were funded by City of Melbourne grants. I thank them for their support. In particular, the enthusiasm of Candy Mitchell has been of great encouragement. Access to the City of Melbourne collections was generously and professionally assisted by Eddie Butler-Bowdon, Catherine Hockey and Sahra Milk.

The images presented in this book are integral to the storytelling. The photographers who generously gave their time in shooting signage sites include Tim Fluence, Nick Kreisler, Jesse Marlow, Mark Munro, Patrick Rodriguez and Rhiannon Slatter.

Photographers who kindly contributed images from their existing collections include James Boddington, Tim Griffith, Geoff Hocking, Warren Kirk, Trevor Mein, Angus O'Callaghan and Louis Porter.

In addition, the archival photography of Lyle Fowler, Karl Halla, Wolfgang Sievers and Mark Strizic was generously provided through the State Library of Victoria Pictures Collection.

Other individuals who have, in a variety of ways, contributed to this book include:

Peter Atkins, Barbara Beck, Dennis Bryans, Jon Campbell, Jim Cathcart, Jenny Davies, Adam Dimech, Elisabeth Disney, Peter Douglas, Keith Dunstan, the junior models of the Eid family, Juan Ford, Dame Phyllis Frost, Samuel Furphy, Helen Garner, Andrew Haig, Michelle Hamer, Geoff Hocking, Pieter Huveneers, Robert Ingelsberger, Paul Kelly, Carrie Kennedy, Peter Kennedy, Neil Lorimer, Patricia Lovell, Richard Lowenstein, Ben Morrieson, Walter Portelli, Craig Rossetti, Emma Scally, Chris Schilling, Amy Turner, Joyce Wille and Lucy Wilson.

Many organisations also contributed to this project. These include:

Rick Charylo, Able Demolitions & Excavations; Vilma Santoro, Apex Belting; Amanda Wallace, Neil Masterton, Ian McDougall, ARM; Csaba Banki, Cato Purnell Partners; Alli Coster, Clare Johnston, City of Moreland; Amanda Neilson, City of Yarra; Paolo Baracchi, CoAsIt Italian Historical Society; Scott Brodie, Coniston Designs; Dean & Nevin Phillips, Delta Neon; John Denton, Kirsten Trengrove, Denton Corker Marshall; Andrew Budge, Designland; Sue Dight, Events Management Australia; Francis Maurice Design; Don Williams, Global Art Projects; Paul Hede, Hede Architects; David Wixted, Heritage Alliance; Michelle Tapp, JGL Investments; John Wardle, Amanda Ritson, John Wardle Architects; Ben Albrecht, Kozminsky Gallery; David Kilderry, Lunar Drive-In; Corbett Lyon, Lyon Housemuseum; Natasha Skunca, Make Me Iconic; Matt the Maintenance Man, Manchester Unity Building; Steve Grimwade, Melbourne Writers Festival; Leanne O'Shea, Moreland Energy Foundation; Gregory Cope, National Archives of Australia; Julia Ozanjak, Mark Patullo, National Gallery of Victoria; Ann Gibson, Tracey Avery, National Trust of Australia (Victoria); Pat Grainger, Port Melbourne Historical & Preservation Society; Stephen Horsley, Propellant; Mark Poulier, Poulier & Poulier; David Langdon, Richmond & Burnley Historical Society; Vicki Court, Gerardine Horgan, David Thompson, John Rose, Royal Historical Society of Victoria; Bronwyn Clarke, RMIT University; Dorothy Lobert, St Kilda Historical Society; Kevin M Gange, Silver Top Taxi Service; Amy Turner, Smile Solutions; Kate Rhodes, State of Design Festival; Naomi Milgrom, Michele Cooper-Hede, Sussan Group; Lina Favlin, The Fitzroy History Society; Michele Iorio, Touch of Paris; Andrew May, Philip Goad, Mark Davis, University of Melbourne; and Lance Pritchard, Werribee and District Historical Society.

Thank you to my design assistant, Lan Huang, for his supportive photography and the myriad of design aspects of this book.

A special thank you to Erica Downward whose research into the Allen's sign was both exhaustive and inspirational. Likewise, the vision of Patricia Hocking in providing information on the State Savings Bank Girl has brought this sign back into the public eye.

The extraordinary stories from Ian (Podgey) Rogers added a real colour to the project. Many thanks for bringing such richness to the pages.

Inspiration throughout the project was found in many interesting places. These included the sharp wit of Robin Boyd, the vision of Herbert Spencer and the sounds and thoughts of Brian Eno.

Above all, the infinite support of my partner, Christine Eid has enabled this book to have the depth, detail and quality such stories deserve. Her tireless assistance, from the first conversations many years ago right through to production, has made this book possible, so I thank her immensely.

OPPOSITE
Flinders Street Railway
Station crowned and
illuminated for the
Queen's visit (1954)
Mark Strizic
negative, flexible base
*Image: State Library of
Victoria Pictures Collection*
H2008.11/918

OPPOSITE
A rather zesty sign for *Tex-ture brick* cladding, (c.1950s) claiming a heritage as early as 1854, the era of the Melbourne goldrush. The claim was then covered over (see bottom right corner). *Image: Author's Collection*

Select Bibliography

Books

Annear R., *A City Lost & Found: Whelan the Wrecker's Melbourne*, Black Inc., Melbourne, 2005.

Annear R., *Bearbrass: Imagining early Melbourne*, Black Inc., Melbourne, 2005.

Baines P. & Dixon C., *Signs: Lettering in the environment*, Laurence King, London, 2008.

Banham S., *Characters & Spaces: 1 city block 17 stories*, RMIT University, Melbourne, 2009.

Barber S., *Sidney Myer: A life, a legacy*, Hardie Grant Books, Prahran, 2005.

Bartram A., *Lettering in Architecture*, Lund Humphries Publishers, London, 1975.

Bell J., *Lighting Up Australia: The story of the Australian match manufacturing industry 1843-2003*, Jerry Bell, Armadale, 2008.

R. Boyd, *The Australian Ugliness*, Melbourne, Melbourne University Press, 1960

Bryant & May (firm), *The Matchmakers: A story of real life*, Bryant & May, Richmond, 1925.

Cabin C., *A Fine Line: A history of Australian commercial art*, Hale & Iremonger, Sydney, 1983.

Cato K., *Design by Thinking*, Craftsman House, North Ryde, NSW, 2000.

Church J., *Per L'Australia: The story of Italian migration*, Miegunyah Press, Carlton, 2005.

Davison G., *Car Wars: How the car won our hearts and conquered our cities*, Allen & Unwin, Crows Nest, NSW., 2004.

Derham G.A (ed.), *The First Hundred Years 1854-1954: Swallow & Ariell Ltd*, Troedel & Cooper, Port Melbourne, 1954.

Downward E., *The Sweetest of Them All: The history of the Allen's neon sign*, St Kilda, 1987.

Draffin N., *The Art of M. Napier Waller*, Sun Books, South Melbourne, 1978.

Edquist H., *Frederick Romberg: The architecture of migration 1938-1975*, RMIT University Press, Melbourne, 2000.

Fry T., *Design History Australia*, Hale & Iremonger, Sydney, 1988.

Furphy S., *Dimmeys of Richmond: The rise and fall of a family business*, Hyland House, Flemington, 2007.

Goad P., *Melbourne Architecture*, The Watermark Press, Boorowa, N.S.W., 2009.

Gray N., *Lettering on Buildings*, Architectural Press, London, 1960.

Grossi G. & McGuinness J., *Grossi Florentino: Secrets & recipes*, Lantern, Camberwell, 2007.

Hewat T., *The Plastics Revolution: The story of Nylex*, Macmillan, South Melbourne, 1983.

Hocking G., *Signs of the Times: A nostalgic celebration of Australian advertising signs*, Five Mile Press, Rowville, 2005.

Hunter M., *Australia Post Delivering More Than Ever*, Focus Publishing, Edgecliff, NSW., 2000.

Kinneir J., *Words and Buildings: The art and practice of public lettering*, Architectural Press, London, 1980.

Kirkham C., *Margarine: Seed oils replace nuts. The history of Nuttelex*, Nuttelex Food Products Pty Ltd, Prahran, 2000.

Lewis M., *Melbourne: The city's history and development*, City of Melbourne, Melbourne, 1995.

Longmire A., *St. Kilda the Show Goes On: The history of St Kilda Vol. III, 1930 to July 1983*, Hudson Publishing, Hawthorn, 1989.

Matthews E., *Mark Strizic: Melbourne marvellous to modern*, Thames & Hudson, Fishermans Bend, 2009.

MacRobertsons (firm), *A Young Man and a Nail Can: An industrial romance*, MacRobertson, Melbourne, 1921.

McKay J., *The Rosella Story 1895-1963*, Rosella Preserving Co., North Melbourne, 1977.

McLaughlin J., *Nothing Over Half a Crown: A personal history of the founder of the G.J. Coles stores*, Loch Haven Books, Main Ridge, Vic., 1991.

Marshall A., *The Gay Provider: The Myer story*, F.W. Chesire, Melbourne, 1961.

Myer (firm), *The History of the Napier Waller Murals*, Myer Stores Ltd, Melbourne,1994.

Otto K., *Capital: Melbourne when it was the capital city of Australia 1901-27*, Text Publishing, Melbourne, 2009.

Pelaco (firm), *Pelaco: A visual history of the Pelaco company and brand a century down the track*, Bounce Books, Melbourne, 2006.

Rhodes K., *Melbourne Unbuilt*, National Design Centre Melbourne 2008

Robertson J., *MacRobertson: The chocolate king*, Lothian Books, South Melbourne, 2004.

Robertson J., *MacRobertsonland*, Arcade Publications, Melbourne, 2010.

U. Rondinone U., *Our Magic Hour*, Museum of Contemporary Art, Sydney, 2003.

Stern R., *The New Let There be Neon*, H.N. Abrams, New York, 1988.

Stephens A., Goad P. & McNamara A., *Modern Times: The untold story of modernism in Australia*, Miegunyah Press, Carlton, 2008.

Tout-Smith D., *Melbourne: A city of stories*, Museum Victoria, Melbourne, 2008.

Venturi R., Scott Brown D. & Izenour S., *Learning from Las Vegas: The forgotten symbolism of architectural form*, MIT Press, Cambridge, Massachusetts, 1977.

Vinegar A. & Golec M. (ed.), *Relearning from Las Vegas*, University of Minnesota Press, Minneapolis, 2008.

Webber K., Hoskins I., & McCann J., *What's in Store? A history of retailing in Australia*, Powerhouse Publishing, Sydney, 2003.

Wixted D., *Historic Electric Signage in Victoria*, Heritage Alliance, North Melbourne, 2002.

Journal articles

'A new hotel in Melbourne', *Architecture and Arts*, November 1956, pp. 16-18.

'Bluey Diamond and the hansom cab', *Taxi Talk*, Nº 491, September 2008, pp. 22-23.

P. Goad, 'Best Overend – Pioneer modernist in Melbourne', *Fabrications*, no. 6, June 1995, pp. 101-124.

'Large electric sign in Melbourne', *Australasian Electrical Times*, 27 July 1922, p. 387.

'Re-presenting the City: Cocks, Carmichael, Whitford's Centreway Arcade, Collins Street, Melbourne, 1984-87', *Transition: Discourse on architecture*, no. 22/23, Summer 1987, pp. 80-83.

'The flying kangaroo', *Design World*, no. 6, 1984, pp. 54-57.

Influential books

Altaió V., *Lanfranco Bombelli: US Trade Centre Graphics in Europe*, Arts Santa Monica Department de Cultura i de Communicació, Generalitat de Catalunya, 2009.

Button J. (ed.), *Look Here! Considering the Australian Environment*, Lectures from the Victorian Fabian Society, F.W. Cheshire, Melbourne, 1968.

Cozzolino M. & Fysh Rutherford G., *Symbols of Australia*, Cozbrook, Coburg, 1980.

Hofstede D., *Les Mason: Epicurean Magazine 1966-1979*, The Narrows, Melbourne, 2011.

Janser A., *Typotecture: Typography as architectural imagery*, Lars Müller, Zurich, 2002.

Johnston G., *The Australians*, Rigby, Sydney, 1972.

Poynor R., *Typographica*, Laurence King, London, 2001.

A
TEX-TURE BRIC
RENOVATION
TO LAS
LIFETIME
by
LIFETIME HOME
IMPROVEMENTS PTY. LTD.
392A ST. KILDA RD. MELB.
Phone 26·3368
OR APPLY WITHIN.
BETWEEN THE WORLD AND THE WEATHER
1854

Index

PAGE 272
As a passionate Christian evangelist, Desmond Hynes has created his own unique typographic language (1996)
Warren Kirk
Image: Courtesy of the artist